Power Maths

Year 3
Practice Book 3A

White

CW00342537

What do you look like?
Draw yourself doing your favourite activity.

This book belongs to _Helena_ .

My class is _3R_ .

Series editor: Tony Staneff

Lead author: Josh Lury

Consultants (first edition): Professor Liu Jian and Professor Zhang Dan

Written by Tony Staneff and Josh Lury

Pearson

Contents

This looks like a good challenge!

It is time to do some practice!

How to use this book

Do you remember how to use this **Practice Book**?

Use the **Textbook** first to learn how to solve this type of problem.

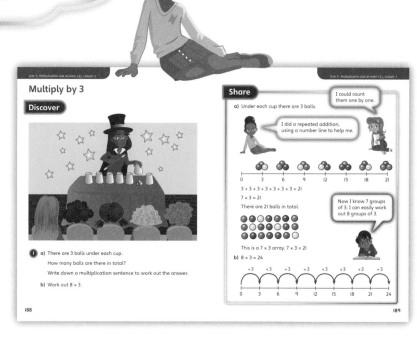

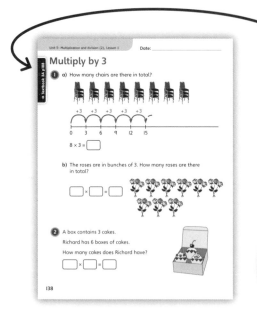

This shows you which Textbook page to use.

Have a go at questions by yourself using this **Practice Book**. Use what you have learnt.

Challenge questions make you think hard!

Questions with this light bulb make you think differently.

Reflect

Each lesson ends with a **Reflect** question so you can think about what you have learnt.

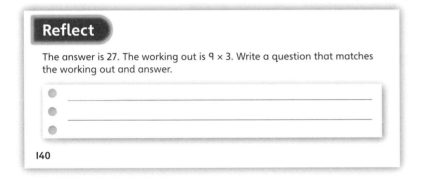

Use **My power points** at the back of this book to keep track of what you've learnt.

My journal

At the end of a unit your teacher will ask you to fill in **My journal**.

This will help you show how much you can do now that you have finished the unit.

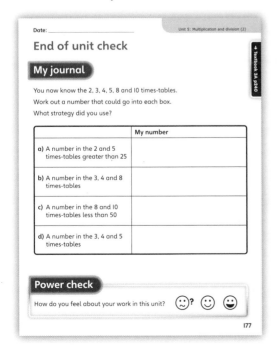

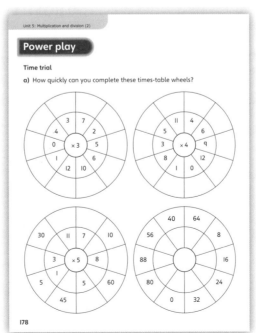

Date: _____

Represent and partition numbers to 100

 How many eggs are there?

a)

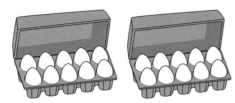  

b)

2 How many milk bottles are there?

3 What numbers are represented with the base 10 equipment?

a)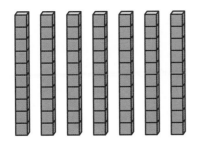

☐

b)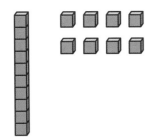

☐

c)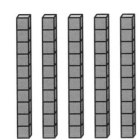

☐

4 Complete the part-whole models.

a)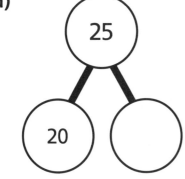

b)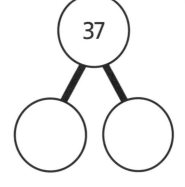

c)

5 Make these numbers with base 10 equipment.

Use the base 10 equipment to complete the part-whole models.

a)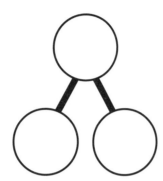

b)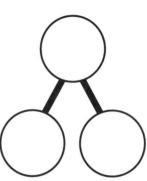

6 Here are three numbers.

Make each number with base 10 equipment.

24 54 84

What is the same about each number?

What is different about each number?

Discuss with a partner.

Reflect

Make a 2-digit number with base 10 equipment.

Draw a part-whole model for your number.

Number line to 100

1 Complete the number lines.

a)

b)
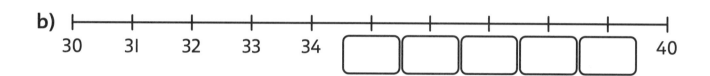

2 What numbers are the arrows pointing to?

a)
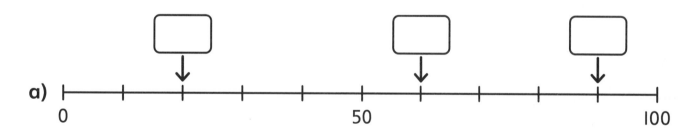

b)
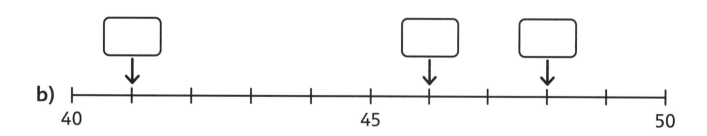

3) What numbers are the arrows pointing to?

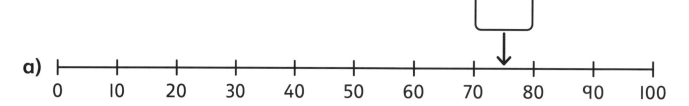

a)

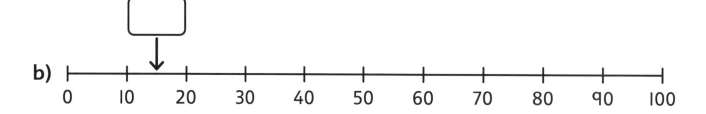

b)

4)

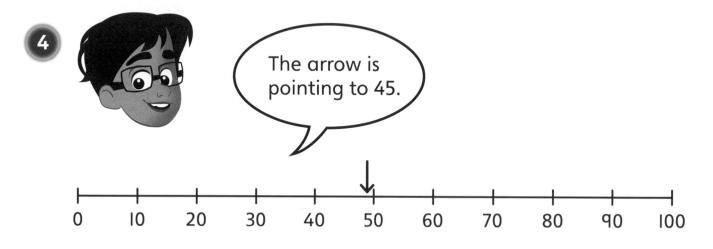

The arrow is pointing to 45.

Do you think Max is correct?

Write the number that the arrow is pointing to.

5) Draw an arrow from each number to its position on the number line.

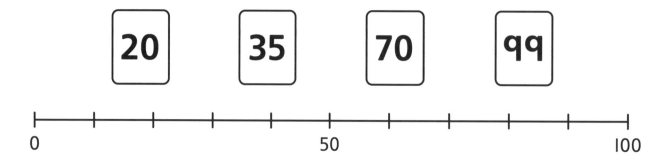

20   35   70   99

6 What numbers are the arrows pointing to?

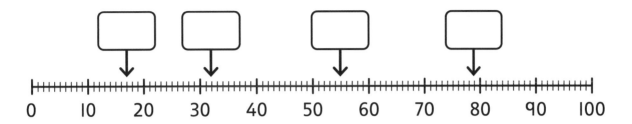

0   10   20   30   40   50   60   70   80   90   100

7 What is the same about all the numbers the arrows are pointing to?

CHALLENGE

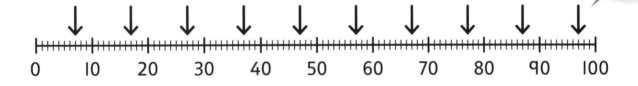

0   10   20   30   40   50   60   70   80   90   100

_____

_____

Reflect

Draw a number line that goes up in 10s.

What numbers is it easy to draw arrows to?

What numbers is it harder to draw arrows to?

Date: _____

100s

1 How many leaflets are in each picture?

a)

☐

b)

☐

c)

☐

2

How many balloons are there?

☐

3 What numbers are shown?

Write your answers in numerals and words.

a)

[ ] _____

b)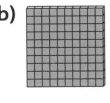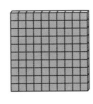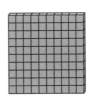

 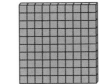

[ ] _____

4 What are the missing numbers?

a)

0	100	200	300			600

b)

1,000			700	600

c) 400, 300, [ ], [ ], [ ]

d) [ ], [ ], 800, 900,

5 A box contains 100 party poppers.

Jamila has 700 party poppers.

Draw how many boxes Jamila has.

6 Andy is counting in 100s.

Seven hundred, eight hundred, nine hundred ...

CHALLENGE

What number should Andy say next?

_____

Reflect

Count out loud from 200 to 1,000 in 100s.

Count out loud from 700 to 0 in 100s.

Did you say any numbers twice? Which ones? _____

Date: 20.9.2022

Represent numbers to 1,000

1 How many sunflower seeds are there?

536

2 How many leaflets are there?

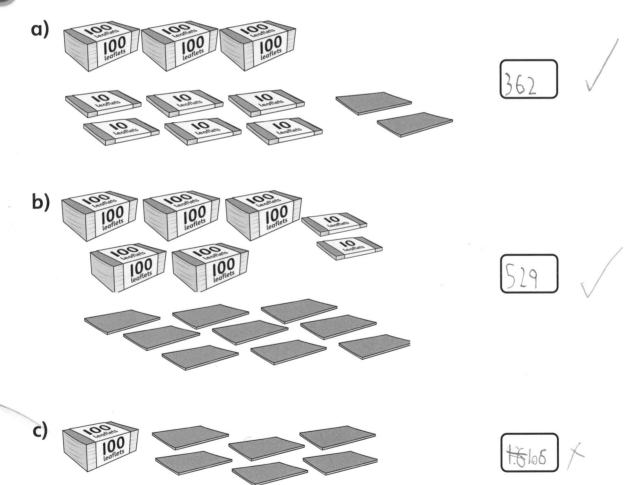

a) 362 ✓

b) 529 ✓

c) 1̶6̶06 ✗

3 Write the numbers shown here.

a)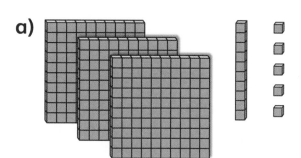

315

b)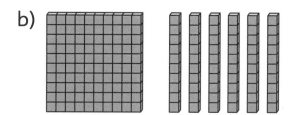

160

c)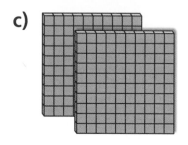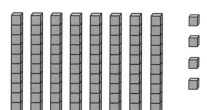

284

d)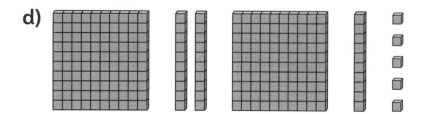

235

4 Make the number 263 with base 10 equipment.

a) How many 100s in 263?

 200

b) How many 10s in 263?

 60

c) How many 1s in 263?

 3

5 Lou makes a 3-digit number with base 10 equipment.

She uses 4 hundreds.

She uses 2 tens.

She uses 9 ones.

What number has she made? 429

6 Olivia has three digit cards.

| 7 | 8 | 2 |

How many different 3-digit numbers can Olivia make?

782   872   287   278   728   827 = 6

Reflect

Write a 3-digit number.

Make your number with base 10 equipment.

How many 100s does it have? How many 10s? How many 1s?

●	500	100	100	200	100	300	= Thousand and 3 hundred									
●																
●																
●																

Date: _____

Partition numbers to 1,000

 1 Complete the part-whole model for each number.

a)

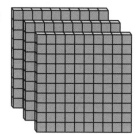 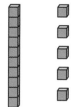

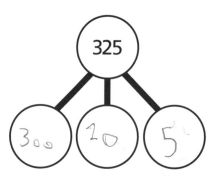

325 = 300, 20, 5

b)

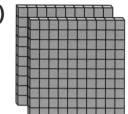

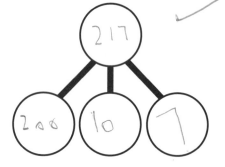

217 = 200, 10, 7

2 Complete the part-whole models.

a)

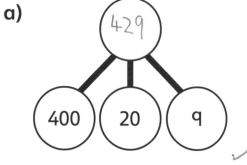

429 = 400, 20, 9

b)

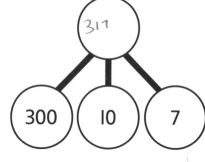

317 = 300, 10, 7

3 Write the numbers that are represented.

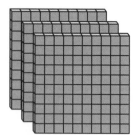 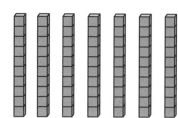

[3] hundreds, [ ] tens and [2] ones is equal to [372].

4 Complete the part-whole models.

a)

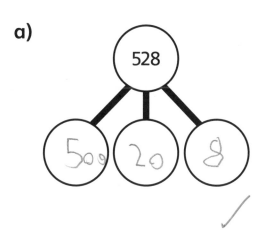

b)

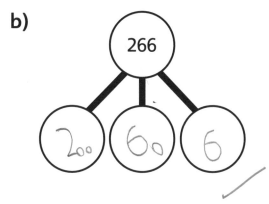

c)

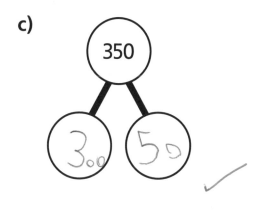

d)

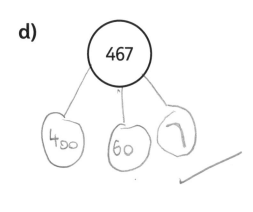

5 Use the part-whole models to complete the number sentences.

a)

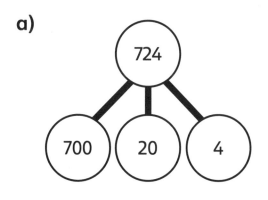

b)

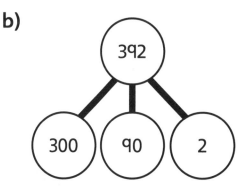

$724 = \boxed{4} + \boxed{20} + \boxed{700}$

$392 = \boxed{2} + \boxed{90} + \boxed{300}$

6 Fill in the boxes to make the calculations correct.

a) 725 = 700 + 20 + [5]

b) 438 = 400 + [30] + [8]

c) 395 = [3] hundreds + [9] tens + [5] ones

d) [700] + [60] = 760

e) 900 + 5 = [905]

7 Fill in the boxes to make the calculations correct. CHALLENGE

a) 7 + 60 + 200 = [267]

d) 457 = 400 + [ ]

b) 5 + 600 + [80] = 658

e) 382 = 300 + 70 + [ ]

c) 38[2] = [3]00 + [8]0 + 2

Reflect

Phil says the answer to this calculation is 468.

Explain why Phil is not correct. He is wrong because it is Swiched round the correct answer is 486.

$$400 + 6 + 80 = ?$$

He is wrong because it is swiched round the

Partition numbers to 1,000 flexibly

1 Complete the part-whole models to show four different ways to partition 352.

a)

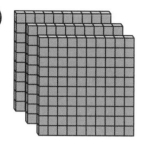
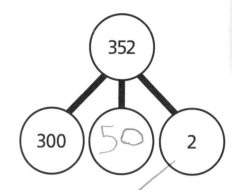

352

300   50   2

b)

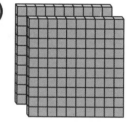
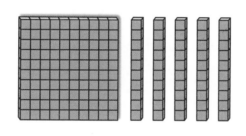
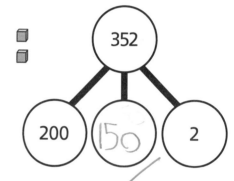

352

200   150   2

c)

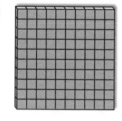
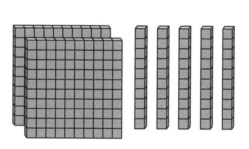
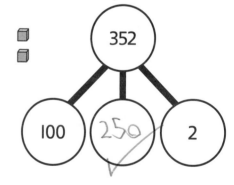

352

100   250   2

d)

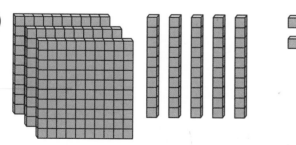
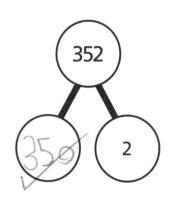

352

350   2

2 Complete the part-whole models to show two different ways to partition 164.

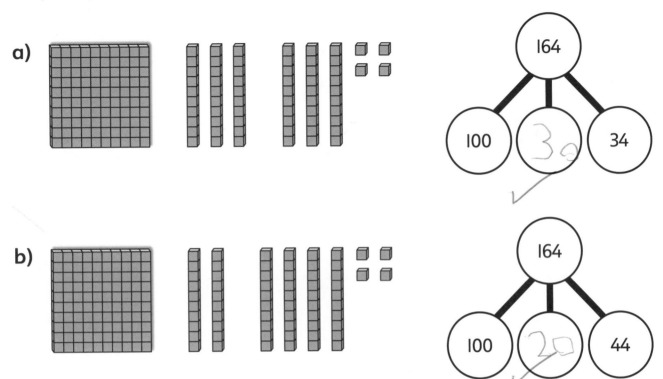

a)

164
100   3̶9̶   34

b)

164
100   2̶0̶   44

3 Complete the part-whole models.

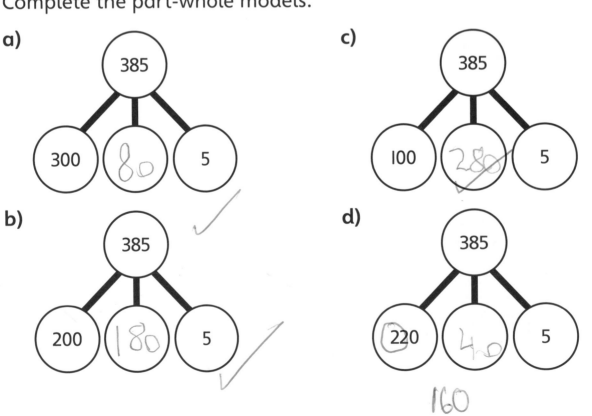

a)

385
300   8̶0̶   5

c)

385
100   2̶8̶0̶   5

b)

385
200   1̶8̶0̶   5

d)

385
220   4̶0̶   5

160

4 What number is represented?

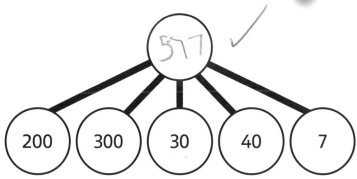

577

200 300 30 40 7

---

5 Fill in the missing numbers.

CHALLENGE

a) $748 = 200 + \boxed{540} + 8$

c) $748 = 400 + \boxed{340} + 8$

b) $748 = \boxed{500} + 240 + 8$

d) $748 = 600 + \boxed{45} + 3$

Reflect

Make the number 524 with base 10 equipment.

Partition the number in three different ways.

Talk to a partner about how you did it.

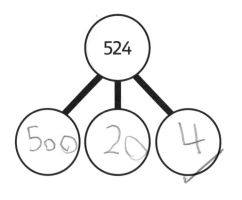

524

500 20 4

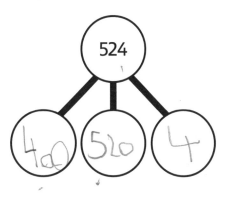

524

400 520 4

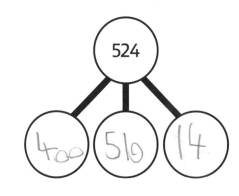

524

400 510 14

Date: 23.9.2022

100s, 10s and 1s

1 What numbers are represented in the place value grids?

a)

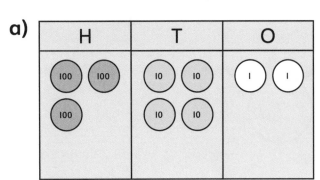

342

c)

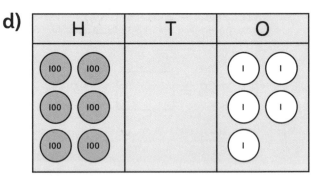

650

b)

H	T	O
100 100	10 10 10 10 10	1 1 1 1 1 1

256

d)

H	T	O
100 100 100 100 100 100		1 1 1 1 1

605

2 Draw counters in the place value grids to represent the numbers.

a) 426

H	T	O
100 100 100 100	10 10	1 1 1 1 1 1

b) 203

H	T	O
100 100		1 1 1

3 Draw counters in the blank place value grids to represent the numbers shown.

a)

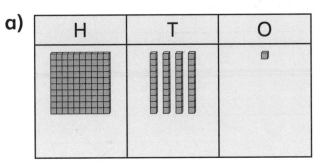

H	T	O
100	10 10 10 10	1

b)

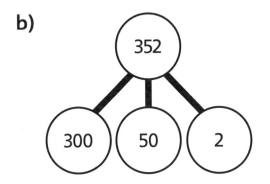

H	T	O
100 100 100	10 10 10 10 10	1 1

4 Tim has 8 blank counters.

He places them on a place value grid.

H	T	O
100 100 100	10 10 10	1 1

a) What number has Tim made?   332

b) He moves a counter from the 100s to the 10s column.

What number has Tim made now?   242

332

CHALLENGE

5 Helen makes this number.

H	T	O
100 100 100	10	1 1 1 1

Ally makes this number.

H	T	O
100 100	10 10 10 10 10 10 10 10 10 10 10	1 1 1 1

Ally and Helen have made the same number. Explain why.

_____

_____

Reflect

Make some numbers in a place value grid using six counters.

How many numbers can you make? Do you think you have made them all?

_____
_____
_____

Date: _____

Use a number line to 1,000

1 How far has each boat travelled?

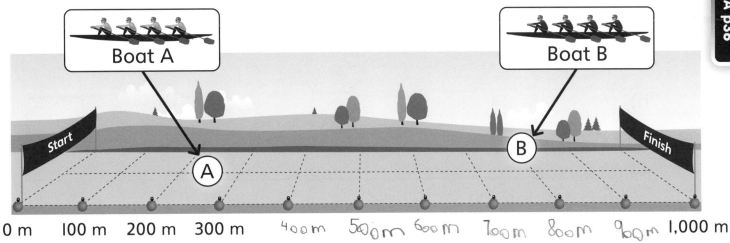

0 m   100 m   200 m   300 m   400 m   500 m   600 m   700 m   800 m   900 m   1,000 m

Boat A has travelled [250 m] metres.

Boat B has travelled [7.8] metres.

2 Fill in the missing numbers.

a)

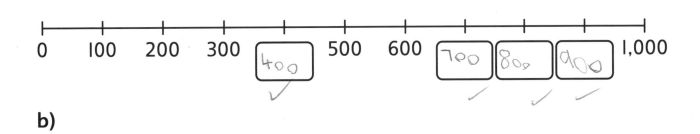

0   100   200   300   [400]   500   600   [700] [800] [900]   1,000

b)

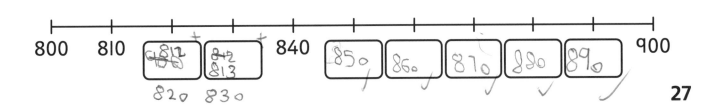

800   810   [812 / 820] [842 / 813]   840   [850] [860] [870] [880] [890]   900

820   830

27

3 What numbers are the arrows pointing to?

a)

205   400   900

| | | | | | | | | | |
0   100   200   300   1,000

b)

440   470   4

400   410   420   500

c)

293   [   ]

280   290

4 Is Isla correct?

I think the arrow is pointing to 101 as it is the next number after 100.

100   200

Explain your answer.

_____

_____

5 Draw arrows to these numbers: 750, 610, 780, 735.

CHALLENGE

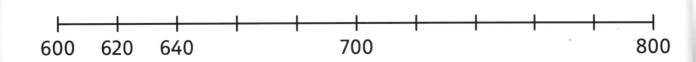

600   620   640   700   800

Reflect

Mark 650 on each number line.

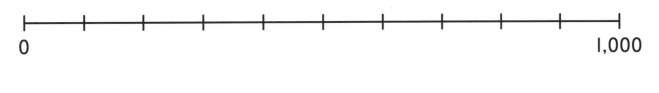

0   1,000

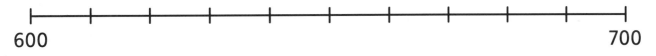

600   700

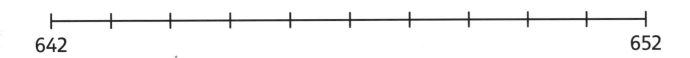

642   652

Why is it **not** in the same place each time?

_____

_____

_____

29

Date: 29.9.2022

Estimate on a number line to 1,000

1. Draw an arrow from each number to its position on the number line.

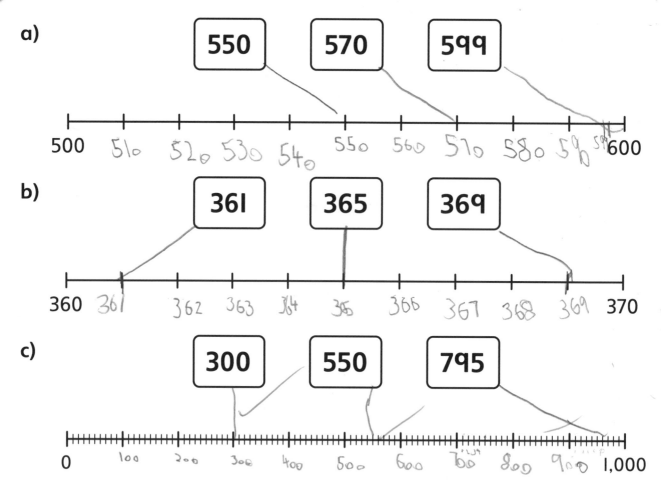

a)

| 550 | 570 | 599 |

500 510 520 530 540 550 560 570 580 590 600

b)

| 361 | 365 | 369 |

360 361 362 363 364 365 366 367 368 369 370

c)

| 300 | 550 | 795 |

0 100 200 300 400 500 600 700 800 900 1,000

2. What numbers could the arrows be pointing to?

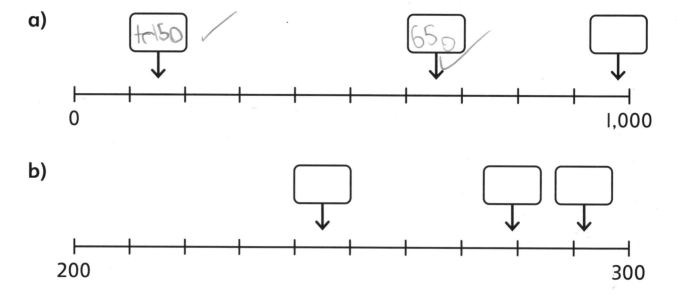

a)

| 150 | | 650 | | |

0 1,000

b)

200 300

3 Write three numbers that come between the two numbers marked.

a)

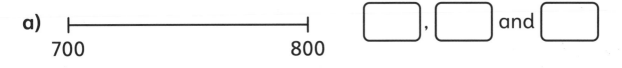

700   800

☐ , ☐ and ☐

b)

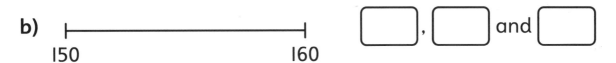

150   160

☐ , ☐ and ☐

4 Estimate the position of each number below. Mark them on the number line.

a)

200   750   998

0   1,000

b)

140   199

100   200

I will divide each number line into 10 equal sections first.

31

5 Mo marks a number on this number line.

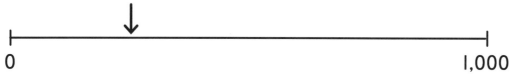

Decide if each statement is true or false or if you cannot tell.

	True	False	Cannot tell
The number is less than 1,000.			
The number is greater than 500.			
The number is less than 700.			
The number ends with a 0.			

Explain to your partner how you know.

6 Complete the start and end numbers on this number line. **CHALLENGE**

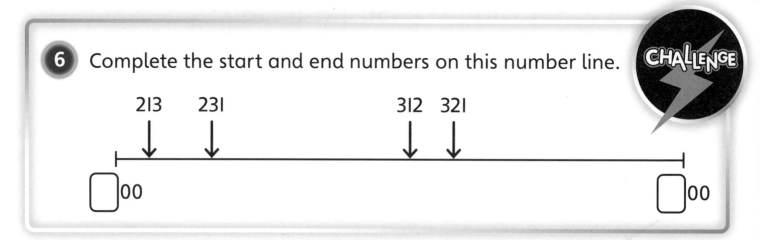

Reflect

Draw a blank number line from 0 to 1,000. Draw an arrow pointing to a position on your number line. What number have you marked?

Find 1, 10 and 100 more or less

1 Tina makes this number.

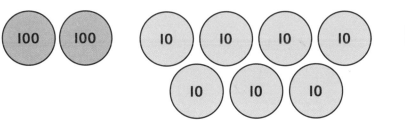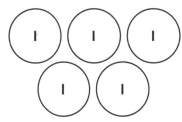

a) What number has Tina made? |275| ✓

b) What is 100 more than Tina's number? |375| ✓

c) What is 10 more than Tina's number? |285| ✓

d) What is 1 more than Tina's number? |276| ✓

2 Here is 482 made with base 10 equipment.

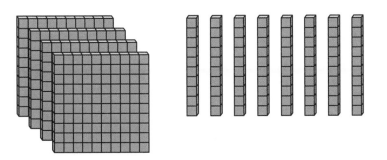

a) What is 100 less than 482? |382| ✓

b) What is 10 less than 482? |472| ✓

c) What is 1 less than 482? |481| ✓

3 Fill in the missing numbers.

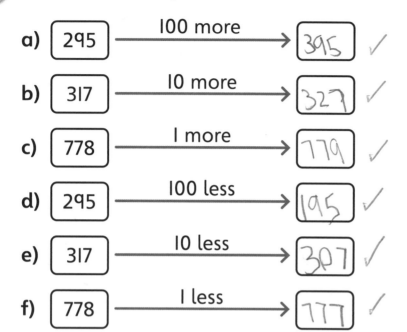

a) 295 — 100 more → 395 ✓

b) 317 — 10 more → 327 ✓

c) 778 — 1 more → 779 ✓

d) 295 — 100 less → 195 ✓

e) 317 — 10 less → 307 ✓

f) 778 — 1 less → 777 ✓

4 a) 10 more than 918 is 928. ✓   d) 100 less than 389 is 289.

b) 100 more than 755 is 855. ✓   e) 10 less than 728 is 718.

c) 1 less than 79 is 78. ✓   f) 1 more than 005 is 115.

5 Mo thinks of a number.

100 more than his number is 598.

a) What is Mo's number? 498

b) Complete the table for Mo's number.

100 more	100 less	10 more	10 less	1 more	1 less
598	498				

6 Can you get from Start to Finish on this board?

You can only move one space at a time and go up, down, left or right.

Start 120	10 more	100 more	1 more
10 more	1 less	1 less	10 more
100 more	10 less	10 less	10 less
100 less	100 more	Finish 309	100 more

7 **a)** 10 more than my number is 345.

What is 100 more than my number?

CHALLENGE

b) What is 10 more than 100 less than 238?

Reflect

Roll three dice and make a 3-digit number:

Complete the table for your number.

100 more	100 less	10 more	10 less	1 more	1 less

Swap tables with a partner and see if you can work out their number. Explain your thinking to your partner.

Date: 4.10.2022

Compare numbers to 1,000

1 **a)** Circle the greater number in each pair.

H	T	O
3	4	8

H	T	O
2	5	1

b) Circle the smaller number in each pair.

H	T	O
3	6	7

H	T	O
3	8	2

2 Circle the greater number in each pair.

a) 278 and 395

d) 377 and 379

b) 495 and 474

e) 711 and 500

c) 400 and 84

f) 704 and 740

3 **a)** Circle the numbers that are less than 430.

450   608   900   53   170   340

b) Circle the numbers that are greater than 285.

290   280   286   285   300   29   1,000

what other number(s)

36

4 Complete using <, > or =.

a)

H	T	O
1	2	9

H	T	O
2	1	0

b)

H	T	O
9	7	0

H	T	O
0	9	7

c) 309 ◯< 320

d) 494 ◯> 409

e) 718 ◯< 1,000

f) 426 ◯= 400 + 20 + 6

5 Write digits in the boxes to make the statements true.

a)

H	T	O
5	6	5

>

H	T	O
5	5	5

b)

H	T	O
5	6	5

<

H	T	O
5	6	9

c) 38 9 > 3 8 7

d) 9 0 1 < 9 5 8

I wonder how many answers there are for some of these.

6 Three children each think of a 3-digit number.

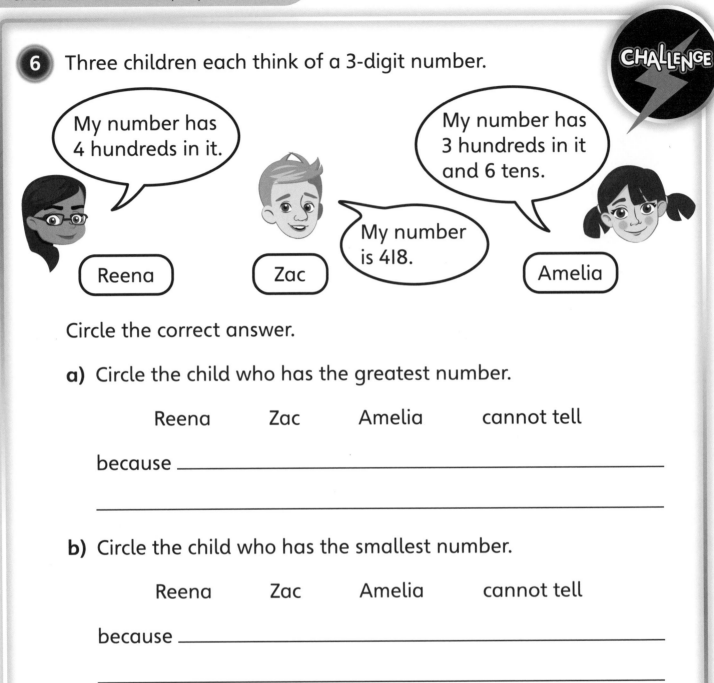

My number has 4 hundreds in it.

Reena

My number is 418.

Zac

My number has 3 hundreds in it and 6 tens.

Amelia

CHALLENGE

Circle the correct answer.

a) Circle the child who has the greatest number.

Reena   Zac   Amelia   cannot tell

because _____

_____

b) Circle the child who has the smallest number.

Reena   Zac   Amelia   cannot tell

because _____

_____

Reflect

Work out which number is greater.

518   514

Discuss all the steps you need to take with a partner.
Use words like first, then, last, 100s, 10s, 1s, compare.

→ Textbook 3A p52

Order numbers to 1,000

1 Here are three towers and their heights.

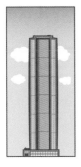 A is 225 m tall

 B is 256 m tall

 C is 180 m tall

Write the heights in order.

Start with the shortest.

	H	T	O
Tower A	2	2	5
Tower B	2	5	6
Tower C	1	8	0

C 180m   , A 225m , B 256m

  shortest   tallest

2 Write the following numbers in order, starting with the greatest.

H	T	O
4	1	7
7	4	0
4	7	1

Write the numbers in order, from smallest to greatest.

417   , 471   , 740

  smallest   greatest

39

3 Here are four jars of counters.

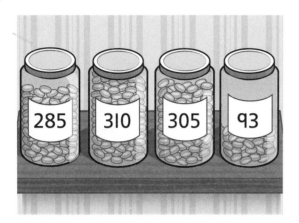

H	T	O
2	8	5
3	1	0
3	0	5
9	9	3

Write the numbers shown on the jars from greatest to smallest.

_310_, _305_, _285_, _93_

greatest   smallest

4 Write each set of numbers in order, starting with the smallest number.

a) | 115 | 126 | 118 |

b) | 295 | 200 | 529 | 207 |

c) | 86 | 800 | 806 | 608 |

| 207 | 295 | | |

d) | 780 | 70 | 80 | 870 |

| | | | |

5 The following numbers are in order.

What could the missing digits be?

Find three possible answers for each one.

CHALLENGE

a) ⬚85 < 39⬚ < ⬚18

⬚85 < 39⬚ < ⬚18

⬚85 < 39⬚ < ⬚18

b) ⬚85 > 38⬚ > ⬚18

⬚85 > 38⬚ > ⬚18

⬚85 > 38⬚ > ⬚18

Reflect

Look at these numbers and then think about how you would put them in order from smallest to greatest.

| 718 | 817 | 78 | 871 |

Explain your method.

_____

_____

_____

Date: 6.10.2022

Count in 50s

1 Each box contains 50 strawberries.

a) Complete the table.

Number of boxes		Number of strawberries
1	🍓50	50
2	🍓50 🍓50	100 ✓
3	🍓50 🍓50 🍓50	150 ✓
4	🍓50 🍓50 🍓50 🍓50	200 ✓
8	🍓50 🍓50 🍓50 🍓50 🍓50 🍓50 🍓50 🍓50	400 ✓
10	🍓50 🍓50 🍓50 🍓50 🍓50 🍓50 🍓50 🍓50 🍓50 🍓50	500 ✓

b) Circle 550 strawberries.

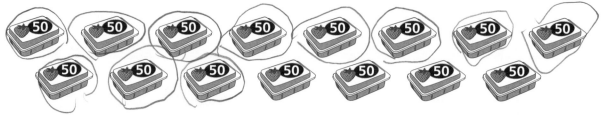

2 Fill in the missing numbers.

a)

0	50	100	150	200	250	300	350

b)

500	550	600	650	700	750	800	850	900

c)

200	250	300	350	400	450	500

d)

700	650	600	550	500	450	400	350	300

3 Eko and Allie are playing a game.

What numbers are covered by the circle and the triangle?

⬤ = 250

▲ = 600

0	50	100	150	200

				250

500	450	400	350	300

550

▲	650	700	750	800

4 Nails are sold in large boxes of 100 and smaller boxes of 50.

How many nails are there in total?

a)

400

450 ✓

b)

500 550 ✓

5 How many 50p coins in £7?

14

£1 = 100p

CHALLENGE

50 100 150 200 250

0 ... ...

75 ... 600 65

Reflect

Count in 50s from 0 to 1,000.

Can you see a pattern in the numbers? Explain your answer.

_____

_____

_____

_____

Date: _____

End of unit check

My journal

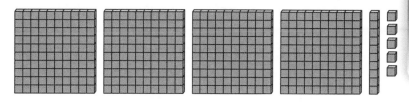

→ Textbook 3A p60

1 What number is shown?

Represent and draw the number in different ways.

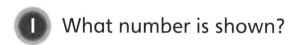

Find five ways to describe the number using as many keywords as you can.

Keywords

hundreds, tens, ones, more, less, number line, between

_____

_____

_____

_____

_____

_____

2 Here are seven counters.

H	T	O

How many numbers can you make that are greater than 500 but less than 700?

You must use all the counters.

What happens if you have eight counters?

_____

_____

_____

Power check

How do you feel about your work in this unit?

Power play

You will need: a place value grid (HTO) and six blank counters.

Place all the counters on the place value grid to make a number.

H	T	O

Using all your counters, find 3-digit numbers to complete the table.

	Largest number you can make
	Smallest number you can make
	An odd number greater than 200
	An even number less than 200
	A number that has the same number of 100s and 1s
	A number where 10 more is 241

Write all your numbers on the number line.

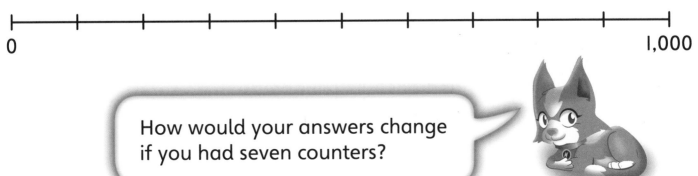

0   1,000

How would your answers change
if you had seven counters?

Date: 7.10.2022

Use known number bonds

1 Complete the additions.

a)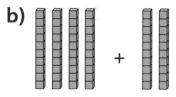

4 ones + 2 ones = 6 ones ✓

b)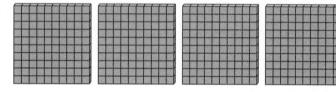

4 tens + 2 tens = 6 tens ✓

c)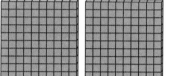

4 hundreds + 2 hundreds = 6 hundreds ✓

2 Complete the subtractions.

a)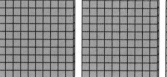

7 ones − 3 ones = 4 ones ✓

b)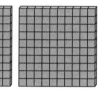

7 hundreds − 3 hundreds = 4 hundreds ✓

3 Complete the addition.

a)

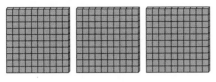 +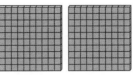

$\boxed{3}00 + \boxed{2}00 = \boxed{5}00$ ✓

b) Complete the subtraction.

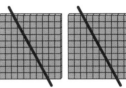

$700 - \boxed{6}00 = \boxed{1}00$

4 Complete these additions and subtractions.

a) $3 + 5 = \boxed{8}$ ✓

$300 + 500 = \boxed{80}$ ✗

b) $4 + 4 = \boxed{8}$ ✓

$400 + 400 = \boxed{800}$ ✓

c) $8 + 1 = \boxed{9}$ ✓

$800 + 100 = \boxed{900}$ ✓

d) $6 - 4 = \boxed{2}$ ✓

$600 - 400 = \boxed{200}$ ✓

e) $9 - 7 = \boxed{2}$ ✓

$900 - 700 = \boxed{200}$ ✓

f) $10 - 6 = \boxed{4}$ ✓

$1,000 - 600 = \boxed{400}$ ✓

5 Complete these additions and subtractions.

a) $700 - 200 = \boxed{500}$ ✓

b) $500 - 200 = \boxed{300}$ ✓

c) $700 - \boxed{500} = 200$ ✓

d) $700 + 200 = \boxed{900}$ ✓

e) $500 + \boxed{200} = 700$ ✓

f) $500 = \boxed{300} - 200$ ✗

49

6

a) How many ice creams and choc ices are there in total? ⬚

b) The shopkeeper sells 300 drinks.

   How many drinks are left? ⬚

CHALLENGE

7 Crack the code. Each symbol represents a single digit.

⭐ 00 + △ 00 = ⬚ 00

△ 00 − ⭐ 00 = 200

⬚ + △ + ⭐ = 16

⭐ = ⬚   △ = ⬚   ⬚ = ⬚

Reflect

How many addition and subtraction facts for 100s can you write that use the number fact 9 − 4 = 5?

Discuss with a partner.

Date: 10.10.2022

Add/subtract 1s

1 Work out the additions.

a)

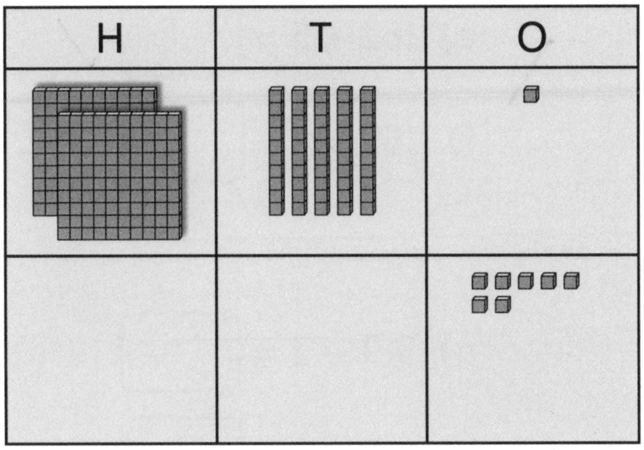

H	T	O

251 + 7 = 258 ✓

b)

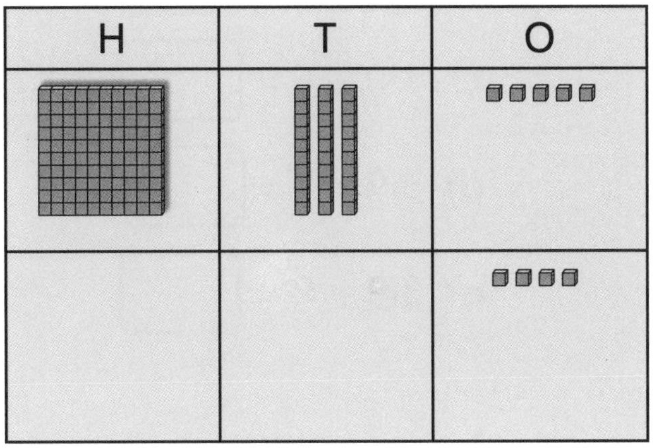

H	T	O

135 + 4 = 139 ✓

2 Work out the subtractions.

a)

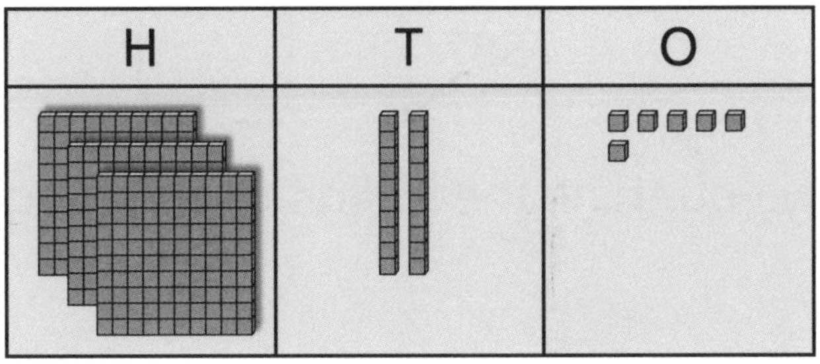

H	T	O

326 − 4 = 322 ✓

b)

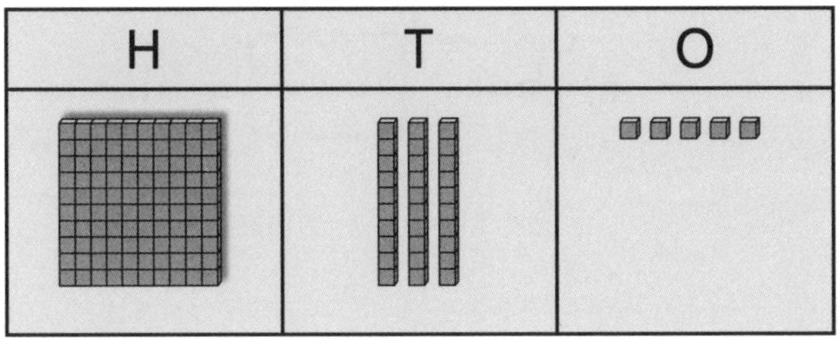

H	T	O

135 − 4 = 131

3 Work out

a) 162 + 1 = 163 ✓

b) 162 + 2 = 164 ✓

c) 162 + 3 = 165 ✓

d) 162 + 4 = 166 ✓

e) 162 + 5 = 167 ✓

f) 162 + 7 = 169 ✓

4 Work out

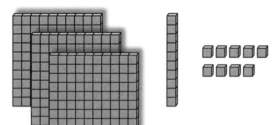

a) 319 − 2 = 317 ✓

b) 319 − 3 = 316 ✓

c) 319 − 6 = 313 ✓

d) 319 − 7 = 312 ✓

e) 319 − 9 = 310 ✓

5 a) Work out

285 + 3 = ☐

317 + 2 = ☐

258 − 3 = ☐

587 − 5 = ☐

b) Discuss with a partner why you think the 1s digit changes each time.

6 Complete the number sentences.

a) ☐ = 315 + 3

b) 200 + ☐ = 207

c) 514 − ☐ = 511

7 Complete the missing digits and numbers.

a) 5 + 123 = ☐

b) 128 = ☐ + 128

c) ☐23 + 5 = 628

d) 638 = 5 + ☐

8 Use the digit cards to complete the number sentences. You may use a card more than once.

| 0 | 1 | 2 | 3 | 4 | 5 | 6 | 7 | 8 | 9 |

1 5 ☐ + ☐ = 1 5 9

5 4 ☐ - ☐ = 5 4 9

4 3 ☐ + ☐ < 4 3 4

Reflect

Show how to solve 235 − 3 and 235 + 3 using equipment or a drawing.

Date: 11.10.2022

Add/subtract 10s

1 Work out the additions.

a)

H	T	O

$236 + 20 = \boxed{256}$ ✓

b)

H	T	O

$152 + 30 = \boxed{182}$ ✓

2 Work out the subtractions.

a)

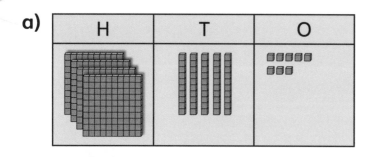

$458 - 30 = \boxed{428}$ ✓

b)

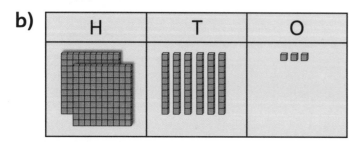

$263 - 50 = \boxed{213}$ ✓

3 Jack has made this number.

a) What number has Jack made? 635 ✓

b) Jack adds 4 more 10s beads.

What number does Jack have now? 665 ✗

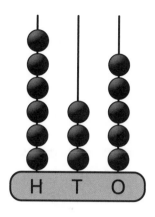

H   T   O

4 Work out

a) 245 + 10 = 255 ✓

245 + 20 = 265 ✓

245 + 30 = 275 ✓

245 + 40 = 285 ✓

245 + 50 = 295 ✓

b) 385 − 10 = 375 ✓

385 − 20 = 365 ✓

385 − 30 = 355 ✓

385 − 40 = 345 ✓

385 − 50 = 335 ✓

Discuss with a partner what you notice.

Which digit changes? Why?

5 Complete the number sentences.

a) 654 + 40 = 694 ✗

b) 654 = 20 − 30 ✗

c) 654 + 20 = 674 ✓

d) 295 − 40 = 255 ✓

e) 654 = 604 + 50 ✓

f) 265 + ☐ = 265 − ☐

6 Reuben makes 4 numbers.

CHALLENGE

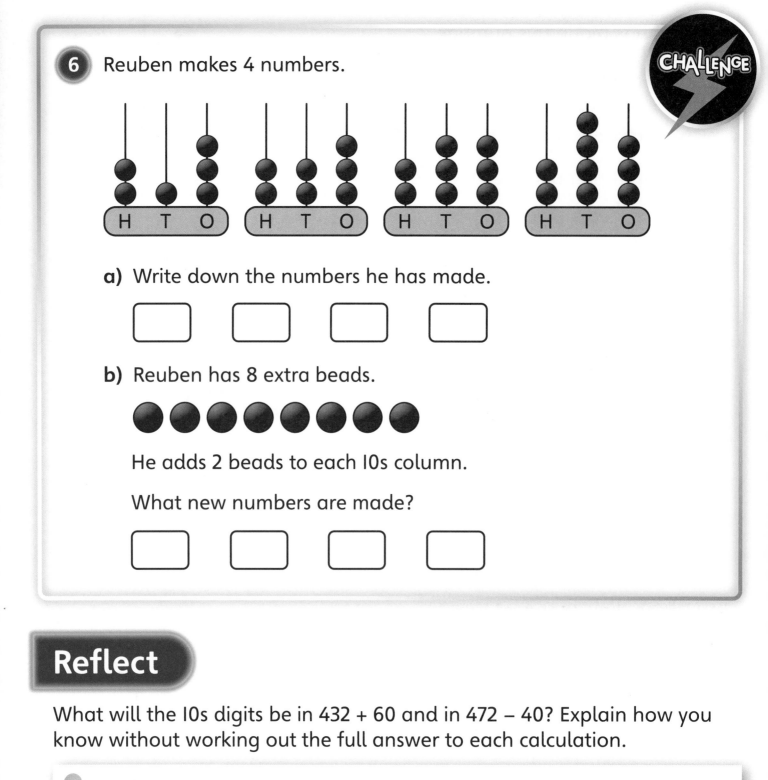

a) Write down the numbers he has made.

b) Reuben has 8 extra beads.

He adds 2 beads to each 10s column.

What new numbers are made?

Reflect

What will the 10s digits be in 432 + 60 and in 472 – 40? Explain how you know without working out the full answer to each calculation.

Date: 12·6·2022

Add/subtract 100s

1 Work out the additions.

a)

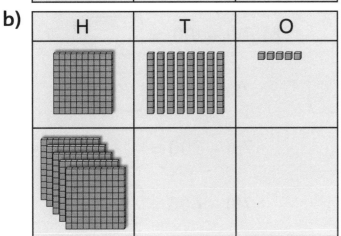

$216 + 300 = \boxed{516}$

b)

$185 + 500 = \boxed{685}$

2 Work out the subtractions.

a)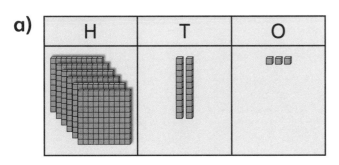

$623 - 200 = \boxed{603}$

b)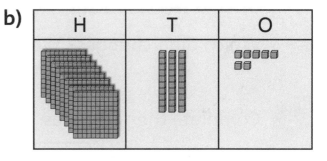

$837 - 500 = \boxed{337}$

3 Here is a number.

H	T	O
100 100 100 100 100	10	1 1 1 1

a) What is 200 more than this number? 714

b) What is 200 less than this number? 314

4 Work out

a) 326 + 100 = 426

   326 + 200 = 526

   326 + 300 = 626

   326 + 400 = 726

   326 + 500 = 826

b) 781 – 100 = 681

   781 – 200 = 581

   781 – 300 = 481

   781 – 400 = 381

   781 – 500 = 281

Discuss with a partner what you notice.

Which digit changes? Why?

5 Complete the sentences.

a) 300 more than ⬚ is 981.

b) 200 less than ⬚ is 65.

6 Alex, Ebo and Kate have some stamps.

CHALLENGE

Alex: I gave 200 stamps to Kate and 100 to Ebo. I have none left now.

Ebo: I gave 400 stamps to Kate and have none left now.

Kate: I have 780 stamps now!

How many stamps did each person have to begin with?

Alex ⬜

Ebo ⬜

Kate ⬜

Reflect

Why don't the 10s and 1s digits change when you add 100s to a number?

Discuss with a partner.

Date: 13.10.2022

Spot the pattern

1 Complete these additions.

Discuss with a partner what you notice.

a) 254 + 4 = 258 ✓

H	T	O

b) 254 + 40 = 294 ✓

H	T	O

c) 254 + 400 = 654 ✓

H	T	O

2 Complete the missing parts of these calculations.

a) 456 − 200 = 256 ✓

H	T	O

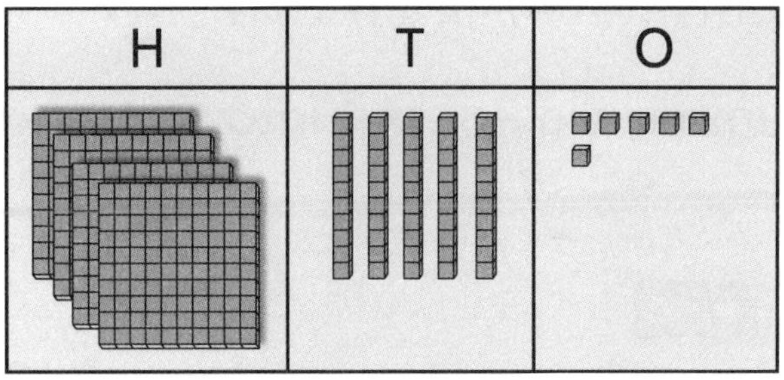

b) 456 − 20 = 476 ⟨m⟩

436

H	T	O

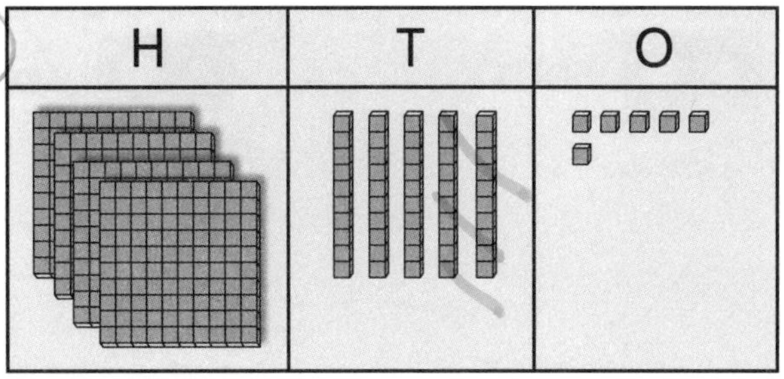

3 Complete these calculations.

a) 345 + 200 = 545 ✓

345 + 20 = 365 ✓

345 + 2 = 347 ✓

b) 757 = 777 − 20

775 = 777 − 2

777 = 979 − 200

977

c) 444 + 30 = 474 ✓

444 + 300 = 744 ✓

444 + 3 = 447 ✓

d) III = 3II ⟨>⟩ III   − 200

III = 4II ⟨>⟩ III

5II = III ⟨<⟩ 5II

4 Zac put the same number into each machine.

The outputs were 791, 737 and 197.

What number did Zac put into the machines?

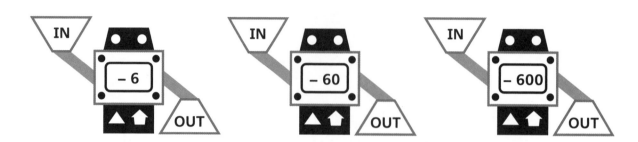

5 Discuss with a partner the mistake Dexter has made.

232 + 20   212 – 200

292 + 20   322 – 90

922 – 200   292 – 20

322 + 90

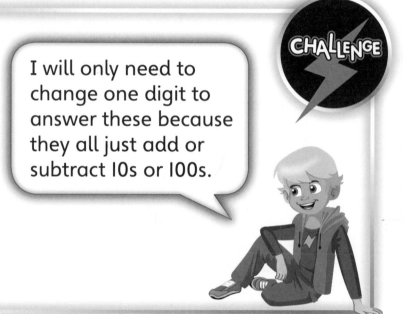

I will only need to change one digit to answer these because they all just add or subtract 10s or 100s.

CHALLENGE

Reflect

Discuss with a partner how you would answer 138 + 20 or 138 + 200 in your head.

Add Is across 10

1 Work out the additions.

a) 318 + 5 = 323

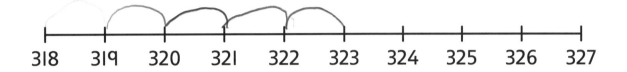

b) 318 + 6 = 324

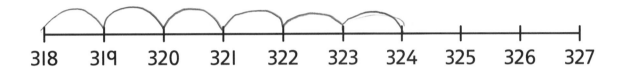

c) 318 + 7 = 325

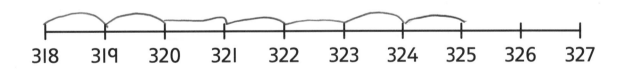

d) 318 + 9 = 327

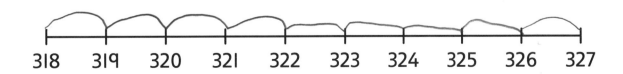

2 Work out the additions.

a) 215 + 7 = 222

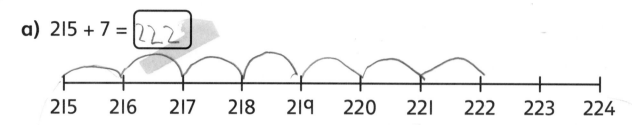

b) 566 + 7 = 573

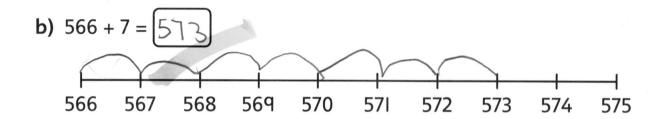

c) 629 + 7 = 636

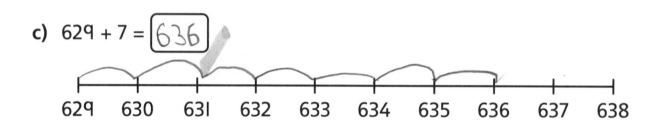

3 Work out the additions.

a) 215 + 8 = ☐

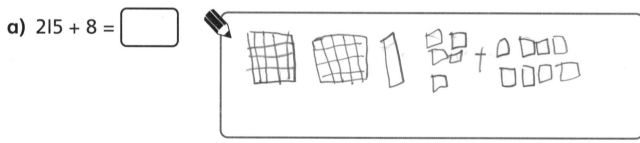

b) 218 + 5 = ☐

c) Discuss with a partner what you notice about your answers to **a)** and **b)**

4 Tick the calculations where the 10s digit will increase.

a)

| 458 + 1 | 185 + 4 | 154 + 8 | 841 + 5 |

| 584 + 1 | 418 + 5 | 514 + 8 | 158 + 4 |

b) Work out the answers to the calculations in your head.

5 Work out the missing numbers.

a) $215 + \boxed{} = 218$

$215 + \boxed{} = 220$

$215 + \boxed{} = 223$

c) $39\boxed{} + 6 = 398$

$39\boxed{} + 6 = 400$

$39\boxed{} + 6 = 403$

b) $\boxed{} + 824 = 830$

$\boxed{} + 824 = 831$

$\boxed{} + 824 = 833$

Reflect

Discuss with a partner what is the same and what is different about how to solve 825 + 3 and 825 + 8.

Date: 18.10.2022

Add 10s across 100

1 Work out the additions.

a) 275 + 60 = 335 ✓

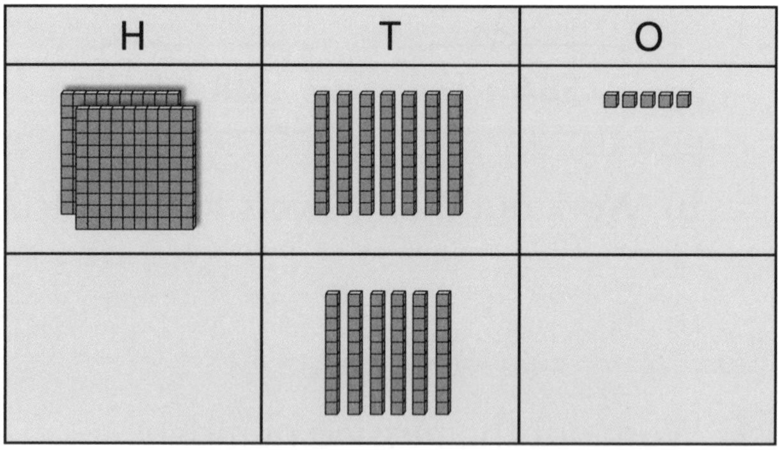

H	T	O

b) 494 + 60 = 554 ✓

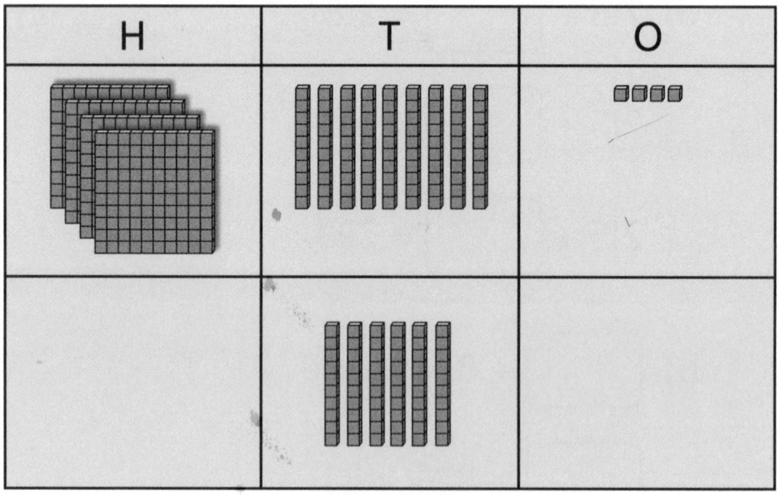

H	T	O

c) 568 + 60 = 628 ✓

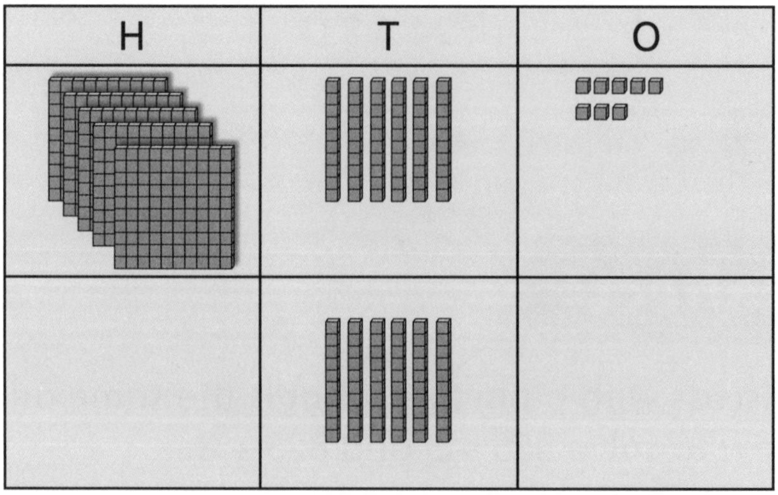

H	T	O

2 Make the number 382 from place value counters.

H	T	O
100 100 100	10 10 10 10 10 10 10 10	1 1

Add these numbers to 382.

a) Add 10   392 ✓

b) Add 20   402 ✓

c) Add 30   412 ✓

d) Add 40   422 ✓

e) Add 80   462 ✓

3 Work out

I notice something about my answers. I wonder why this is.

a) 454 + 70 = 524 ✓

474 + 50 = 524 ✓

b) 593 + 60 = 653 ✓

563 + 90 = 653 ✓

4 What mistake has Isla made?

80 + 538
8 tens + 3 tens = 11 tens
80 + 538 = 518

_____

_____

_____

_____

5 Complete the missing numbers.

a) $234 + 90 = \boxed{}$

b) $371 + 50 = \boxed{}$

c) $\boxed{} = 40 + 569$

d) $20 + \boxed{} = 319$

e) 50 more than 762 is $\boxed{}$

f) $150 = \boxed{} + 90$

6 Danny is working out $861 + 90$ in his head.

CHALLENGE

I will first add on 40.

I will then add on 50.

a) Work out $861 + 90$ using Danny's method. $\boxed{}$

b) Tell a partner a different way to work out $861 + 90$.

Reflect

When I add a 3-digit number and 10s, I know I will need to

exchange 10 tens for 1 hundred if ... _____

_____

_____

Subtract 1s across 10

1 Work out the subtractions.

a) 412 – 3 = 409 ✓

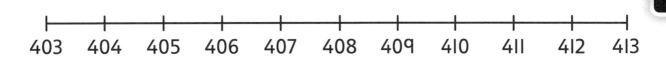

b) 412 – 5 = 407 ✓

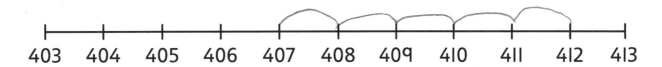

c) 412 – 6 = 406 ✓

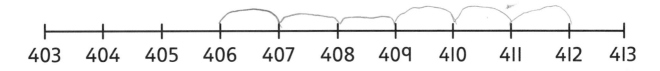

d) 412 – 8 = 404 ✓

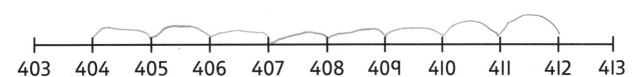

2 Work out the subtractions.

a) 245 – 7 = 238 ✓

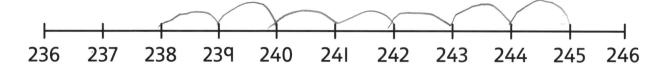

b) 764 – 7 = 757 ✓

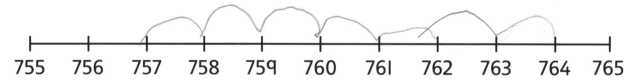

c) 431 – 7 = 424 ✓

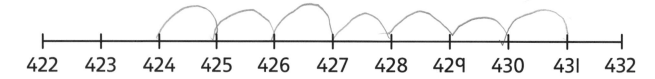

3 Work out the subtractions.

a) 643 – 6 = 637

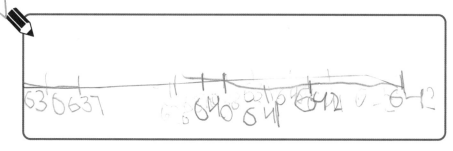

b) 926 – 8 =

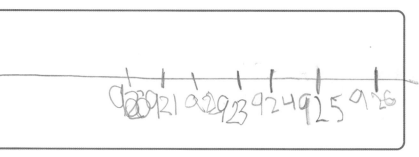

4

235 – 7 = ?
7 ones – 5 ones = 2 ones
235 – 7 = 232
That can't be right?

Explain Isla's mistake and describe how to solve the subtraction.

_____

_____

_____

5 **a)** Work out the missing numbers.

CHALLENGE

174 – ⬚ = 171   174 – ⬚ = 168

174 – ⬚ = 170   174 – ⬚ = 165

b) Work out the missing digits.

35⬚ – 7 = 344   35⬚ – 7 = 345

35⬚ – 7 = 349   35⬚ – 7 = 350

Reflect

Discuss with a partner how you know when the 10s digit of an answer will change when you subtract 1s.

Date: 31.60.2022

Subtract 10s across 100

1 Work out the subtractions.

a)

H	T	O

225 – 50 = 175 ✓

I will use base 10 equipment to help me.

b)

H	T	O

231 – 60 = 171 ✓

c)

H	T	O

315 – 80 = 255 ✗

235

2 Make the number 328 on a place value grid with counters.

H	T	O
100 100 100	10 10	① ① ① ① ① ① ① ①

Work out

a) 328 − 10 = 318 ✓

b) 328 − 20 = 308 ✓

c) 328 − 30 = 298 ✓

d) 328 − 50 = 278 ✓

e) 328 − 70 = ☐

3 Find the missing numbers.

30 less	Number	30 more
	215	245
	316	
		300

4 Complete the calculations.

a) 340 − 60 = ☐

b) 821 − 70 = ☐

c) 350 − 60 = ☐

d) ☐ = 831 − 70

73

5 Complete the part-whole model and missing base 10 equipment.
Then complete the calculations.

a)

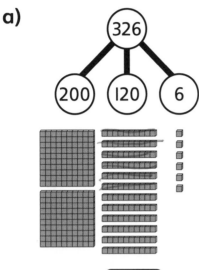

$$326 - 60 = \boxed{266}$$

b)

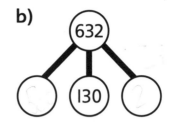

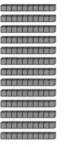

$$632 - 80 = \boxed{}$$

6 Reena thinks of a number. She adds 40 and then adds 50.  CHALLENGE
She ends up with 231. What number did she start with?
Talk to a partner about your method.

231-90   231-100+10=141

Reflect

If you know that 5 + 9 = 14, what other facts can you write?
Discuss with a partner.

90+50=140
5+9=14

Date: 1.11.2022

Make connections

1 Work out

a) 8 + 7 = [15] ✓

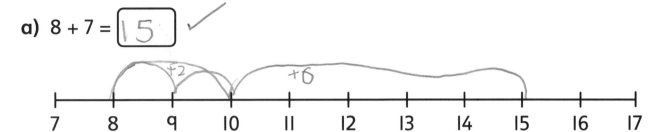

b) 80 + 70 = [150] ✓

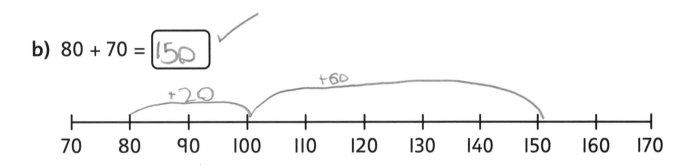

2 Work out

a) 6 + 9 = [15] ✓

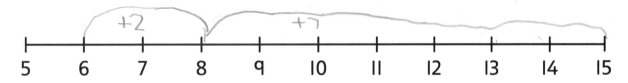

b) 60 + 90 = [150] ✓

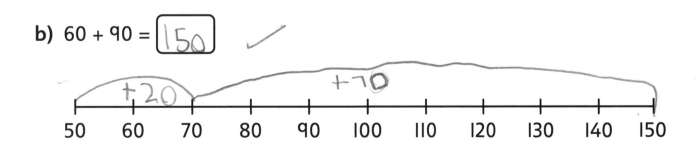

3 Work out

a) 13 − 5 = 8

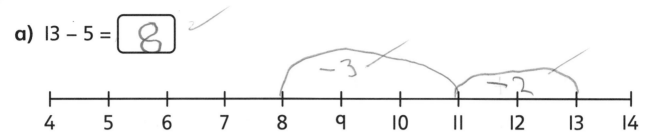

b) 130 − 50 = 80

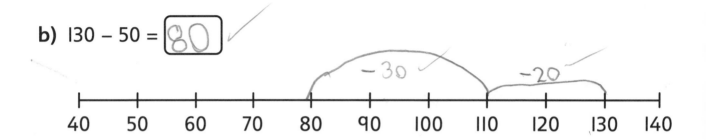

4 Work out

a) 13 − 7 = 6

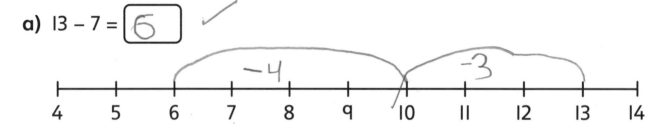

b) 130 − 70 = 60

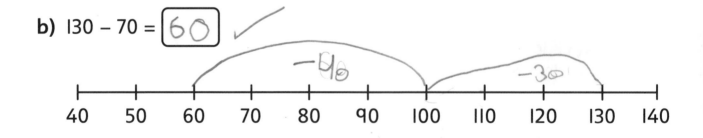

What do you notice about the connection between **a)** and **b)** each time?

5 Aki knows that $18 + 9 = 27$.

Work out

a) $180 + 90 = \boxed{}$

c) $27 - 9 = \boxed{}$

b) $90 + 180 = \boxed{}$

d) $270 - 90 = \boxed{}$

6 Work these out in your head.

CHALLENGE

$\boxed{5 + 8}$ $\boxed{50 + 80}$ $\boxed{150 + 80}$

$\boxed{250 + 80}$ $\boxed{350 + 80}$ $\boxed{750 + 80}$

Discuss your method with a partner.

Reflect

I know $15 - 8$, so I can work out $251 - 80$ by ...

I know that $15-8=7$ $251-80$ $(150+101)$

$251-80+70+100+1=171$

25

77

Date: _____

End of unit check

My journal

→ Textbook 3A p104

Here are two methods for solving the subtraction 548 − 71.

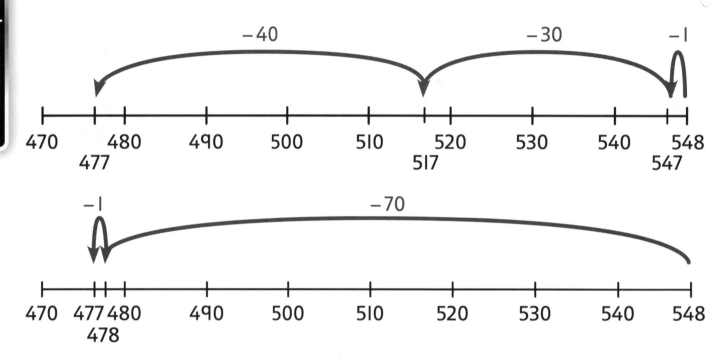

What is the same and what is different about the two methods?

The same is they both take away seventy-one.
The difference is that the first number line
is split into two sections the second is straight.

Power check

How do you feel about your work in this unit?

Power play

Mo is thinking of a 3-digit number.

Kate is thinking of a 2-digit number.

The difference between our numbers is 125.

The sum of our numbers is 201.

Mo

Kate

Try to find their two numbers. You may need to try a few examples. You can use trial and improve.

Keep a record of each attempt you make.

Create a similar puzzle for a partner to solve. What if the difference was 250 and the sum was 402?

Date: 2.11.2022

Add two numbers

1 Complete these additions.

a)

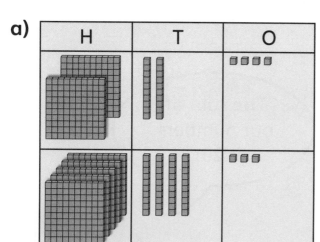

		H	T	O	
		2	2	4	
	+	5	4	3	
		7	6	7	

b)

		H	T	O	
		3	0		
	+	6	4	4	
		9	4	5	

Some of the information is missing from the final place value grid.

2 Find the missing digits.

		H	T	O	
		5	2	7	
	+	2	2	1	
		7	4	8	

3 Complete these additions.

a)

		H	T	O	
		3	4	2	
	+	4	5	6	
		7	9	8	

c)

		H	T	O	
		3	7	4	
	+	4	2	3	
		7	9	7	

e) $704 + 163 = \boxed{867}$

		H	T	O	
		7	0	4	
	+	1	6	3	
		8	6	7	

b)

		H	T	O	
		2	6	0	
	+	7	1	2	
		9	7	2	

d) $311 + 583 = \boxed{894}$

		H	T	O	
		3	1	1	
	+	5	8	3	
		8	9	4	

$374 + 23 =$

374
-23
‾‾‾‾‾

4 There are 235 boys and 312 girls in a school.

How many children are there in total?

235   235   H T O
    + 312   4 2 7
     547 +   5 2
            4 7 9

5 Fill in the missing digits.

a)

		H	T	O	
		1	8	6	
	+	3	1	2	
		4	9	8	

b)

		H	T	O	
		3	0	0	
	+	2	4	5	
		5	4	5	

6 Each of these symbols is used instead of a digit. Work out what digit each symbol stands for.

		H	T	O	
		4	■	★	
	+		▲	■	1
		★	★	7	

▲ = ☐

■ = ☐

★ = 6 ✓

---

7 **a)** Work out 540 + 321.

		H	T	O	
		5	4	0	
	+	3	2	1	

CHALLENGE

I wonder if there is a quick way to work these out.

b) Use your answer to work out the following additions.

540 + 322 = ☐   540 + 331 = ☐

540 + 421 = ☐   321 + 540 = ☐

550 + 321 = ☐   ☐ = 550 + 332

Reflect

Joe has tried to add 454 and 134.

Discuss with a partner the mistakes he has made.

		H	T	O	
		4	5	4	
	+	1	4	3	
		6	9	7	

Date: 3.11.2022

Subtract two numbers

1 Complete the subtractions shown with the base 10 equipment and counters.

a) 678 − 135 = 543

		H	T	O	
		6	7	8	
	−	1	3	5	
		5	4	3	

b) 876 − 3̶5̶1̶ 35 = 841

		H	T	O	
		8	7	6	
	−	0	3	5	
		8	4	1	

2 Work out

		H	T	O	
		7	8	6	
	−	5	3	1	
		2	5	5	

3 Complete these subtractions.

a) 888 − 434 = **454**

		H	T	O	
		8	8	8	
	−	4	3	4	
		4	5	4	

d) 688 − 340 = **348**

		H	T	O	
		6	8	8	
	−	3	4	0	
		3	4	8	

b) 868 − 443 = **425**

		H	T	O	
		8	6	8	
	−	4	4	3	
		4	2	5	

e) 688 − 34 = **654**

		H	T	O	
		6	8	8	
	−	0	3	4	
		6	5	4	

c) 886 − 340 = **546**

		H	T	O	
		8	8	6	
	−	3	4	0	
		5	4	6	

f) **364** = 668 − 304

		H	T	O	
		6	6	8	
	−	3	0	4	
		3	6	4	

4 Find the missing digits from this subtraction.

H	T	O

		H	T	O	
		8	9	4	
	−	6	9	0	
		2	0	4	

84

5 There were 377 people at the cinema and 599 people at a concert.

How many more people were at the concert?

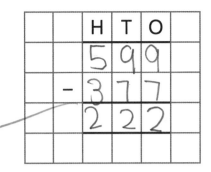

222

6 Use only the digits 0, 1 and 2 to complete each subtraction. Write a number to subtract to make the given answer. Find two solutions to each.

CHALLENGE

a) The answer is between 200 and 220.

333 – ☐☐☐   333 – ☐☐☐

b) The answer is odd.

444 – ☐☐☐   444 – ☐☐☐

c) The answer is a multiple of 5.

☐☐☐ – 101   ☐☐☐ – 101

Reflect

Show how to solve 372 – 251 using base 10 equipment or a drawing.

Date: _____

Add two numbers (across 10)

1 Work out

a) 158 + 124 = 282

		H	T	O	
		1	5	8	
	+	1	2	4	
		2	8	2	
			1		

b) 215 + 137 = 352

		H	T	O	
		2	1	5	
	+	1	3	7	
		3	5	2	
			1		

c) 426 + 346 = 772

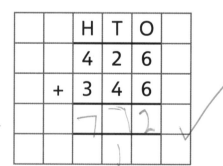

		H	T	O	
		4	2	6	
	+	3	4	6	
		7	7	2	
			1		

2 Work out

a)

		H	T	O	
		2	3	7	
	+	1	4	5	

b)

		H	T	O	
		3	0	5	
	+	5	1	6	

c)

		H	T	O	
		4	6	2	
	+	4	3	8	

3 Set as a column addition.

a) 357 + 127

		H	T	O	
	+				

b) 418 + 523

		H	T	O	
	+				

4 a) Write the missing digits.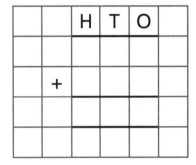

		H	T	O	
		4	7	8	
	+				
		6	9	3	

		H	T	O	
		1	7		
	+		1	3	
		1	9	1	

		H	T	O	
				2	
	+	2		2	
		9	6	1	

b) Find three different solutions.

		H	T	O	
				9	
	+	1			
		9	1	1	

		H	T	O	
				9	
	+		1		
		9	1	1	

		H	T	O	
				9	
	+	1			
		9	1	1	

5 Laura drives 289 km.

After a rest, she drives 136 km more.

How far does she drive in total?

CHALLENGE

6 Henri has worked out 317 + 326.

His answer ends in a 4.

How do you know that Henri is incorrect without seeing his working?

_____

_____

Reflect

Bella is working out 305 + 407. She thinks the answer will have 0 in the 10s column because there are no 10s in 305 or 407.

Explain Bella's mistake.

_____

_____

_____

Date: 8.11.2022

Add two numbers (across 100)

1 Work out

a)

		H	T	O	
		1	6	5	
	+	2	5	3	
		4	1	8	
		1			

H	T	O
100	10 10 10 10 10 10	1 1 1 1 1
100 100	10 10 10 10 10	1 1 1

→ Textbook 3A p120

b) 383 + 460 = **843**

		H	T	O	
		3	8	3	
	+	4	6	0	
		8	4	3	
		1			

d) 245 + 363 = **608**

		H	T	O	
		2	4	5	
	+	3	6	3	
		6	0	8	
		1			

c) 591 + 145 = **736**

		H	T	O	
		5	9	1	
	+	1	4	5	
		7	3	6	
		1			

e) 175 + 230 + 382 = **787**

		H	T	O	
		1	7	5	
		2	3	0	
	+	3	8	2	
		7	8	7	
		1			

2 Work out the missing number.

b	617	
365		252

		H	T	O	
		3	6	5	
	+	2	5	2	
		6	1	7	
		1			

3 Miss Hall buys a TV and a games console.

What is the total cost?

		H	T	O	
		2	7	6	
	+	1	6	3	
		4	3	9	
		1			

 £276

 £163

4 Work out

a) 365 kg + 247 kg = ☐ kg

		H	T	O	
	+				

b) £389 + £389 = £ ☐

		H	T	O	
	+				

5 Work out the missing digits.

		H	T	O	
		5		2	
	+		7		
		9	3	6	

		H	T	O	
		4	2		
	+	2		2	
			1	7	

6 Join the calculations to the bubbles to show if an exchange is needed and then complete the calculations.

		H	T	O	
		2	3	6	
	+	1	5	5	

No exchange needed

		H	T	O	
		2	3	7	
	+	1	7	3	

		H	T	O	
		3	4	7	
	+	2	7	0	

Exchange 10 tens for 1 hundred

		H	T	O	
		4	1	0	
	+	1	9	9	

		H	T	O	
		1	0	9	
	+	1	9	0	

Exchange 10 ones for 1 ten

		H	T	O	
		3	8	8	
	+	1	1	3	

7 In this calculation, you need to exchange twice.

$164 + 2\boxed{}\boxed{}$

What could the missing digits be?

Reflect

Explain to a partner how to add two 3-digit numbers.

Date: 9.11.2022

Subtract two numbers (across 10)

1 Work out

a) 382 − 154 =

228

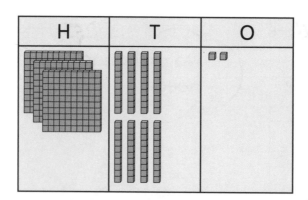

		H	T	O	
		3	8	2	
	−	1	5	4	
		2	2	8	

b) 681 − 235 =

846

	H	T	O
100 100	10 10	1	
100 100	10 10		
100 100	10 10		
	10 10		

Ⓢ

		H	T	O	
		6	8	1	
	−	2	3	5	
		8	4	6	

2 Emma is working out 471 − 135.

Explain Emma's mistake to a partner.

How can you find the correct answer?

		H	T	O	
		4	7	1	
	−	1	3	5	
		3	4	4	

	H	T	O
100 100	10 10	1	
100 100	10 10		
	10 10		
	10		

		H	T	O	
		4	7	1	
	−	1	3	5	
		3	3	6	

3 Work out

a)

		H	T	O	
		9	3²	2	
	−	2	1	5	
			7	7	

b)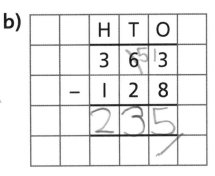

		H	T	O	
		3	6⁵	3	
	−	1	2	8	
		2	3	5	

c)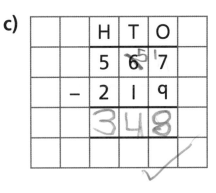

		H	T	O	
		5	6⁵	7	
	−	2	1	9	
		3	4	8	

4 Write these as column subtractions and work out the answers.

a) 354 – 118

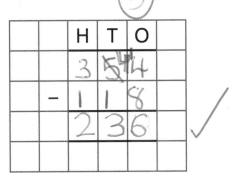

		H	T	O	
		3	5⁴	⁴4	
	−	1	1	8	
		2	3	6	

b) 430 – 208

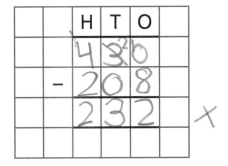

		H	T	O	
		4	3²	⁰0	
	−	2	0	8	
		2	3	2	

5 Work out the missing digits.

a)

		H	T	O	
		5	7	5	
	−	4	4		
		1	3	6	

b)

		H	T	O	
		2		0	
	−		5	3	
		3	4	1	

6 What subtraction is Jacob trying to work out?

Write it as a column subtraction.

H	T	O
(100) (100) (1̶0̶0̶)	(10) (10) (10) (10) (10) (10) (1̶0̶) (1̶0̶) (1̶0̶)	I I I I I I I I̶ I̶ I̶ I̶ I̶ I̶ I̶ I̶

	H	T	O	
−				

7 What do you get if you subtract 263 from the sum of 194 and 195.

Show all the steps in your work.

Reflect

Show a partner the steps to work out 592 − 164.

Date: 14.11.2022

Subtract two numbers (across 100)

1 Work out

a) 328 – 143 = ☐ 185

H	T	O
(100) (100) (100)	(10) (10)	(1)(1)(1)(1)(1) (1)(1)(1)

		H	T	O	
		3	²2	8	
	–	1	4	3	
		1	8	5	✓

b) 715 – 263 = ☐ 452

		H	T	O	
		7⁶	¹1	5	
	–	2	6	3	
		4	5	2	✓

d) 647 – 173 = ☐ 474

		H	T	O	
		6	⁵4	7	
	–	1	7	3	
		4	7	4	

c) 428 – 251 = ☐ 177

		H	T	O	
		4³	¹2	8	
	–	2	5	1	
		1	7	7	

e) 907 – 236 = ☐ 671

		H	T	O	
		9⁸	¹0	7	
	–	2	3	6	
		6	7	1	

2 Work out the missing numbers.

a)

415	
231	184

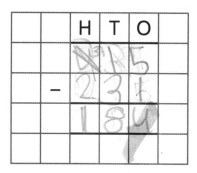

		H	T	O	
		4 1 5			
	−	2 3 1			
		1 8 4			

b)

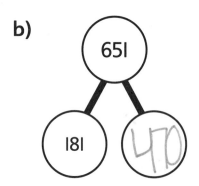

651 — 181 — 470

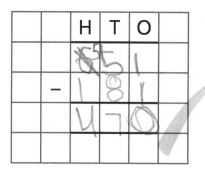

		H	T	O	
		6 5 1			
	−	1 8 1			
		4 7 0			

3 Work out

a) 345 m − 192 m = 153 m

		H	T	O	
		3 4 5			m
	−	1 9 2			m
		1 5 3			m

b) £620 − £340 = £280

		H	T	O	
		£ 6 2 0			£
	−	£ 3 4 0			£
		£ 2 8 0			£

4 546 adults are watching a play.

291 children are watching the play.

How many more adults than children are watching?

245

		H	T	O	
		5 4 6			a
	−	2 9 1			ch
		2 4 5			

X

5 Work out

a) 431 − 276 = 155

		H	T	O	
		4³	³2̸	1	
	−	2	7	6	
		1	5	5	✓

b) 522 − 346 = 176

		H	T	O	
		5	2¹	2	
	−	3	4	6	
		1	7	6	✓

c) 805 − 263 = 542

		H	T	O	
		8̸⁷	0	5	
	−	2	6	3	
		5	4	2	
				✓	

What do you notice about these questions?

The two ones at the start needed exchanging in the tens and ones but the last one was only the tens.

CHALLENGE

6 Two numbers are added to make 828.

One of the numbers is 172.

What is the difference between the two numbers?

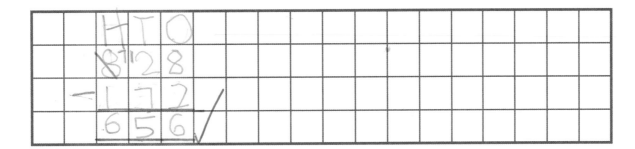

		H	T	O													
		8⁷	¹2	8													
	−	1	7	2													
		6	5	6	✓												

Reflect

Explain to a partner how to subtract any two 3-digit numbers.
What problems might they come across when subtracting?

Date: 16.11.2022

Add a 3-digit and a 2-digit number

1 Work out

a) 168 + 23 = 191

		H	T	O	
		1	6	8	
	+		2	3	
		1	9	1	✓
				1	

b) 183 + 51 = 234

		H	T	O	
		1	8	3	
	+		5	1	
		2	3	4	✓
	1				

2 Complete this addition.

		H	T	O	
		8	2	3	
	+		9	2	
		9	1	5	
		1			✓

3 Complete these additions.

a)

		H	T	O	
		2	5	8	
	+		4	7	
		3	0	5	
			1	1	

b)

		H	T	O	
		3	0	3	
	+		1	7	
		3	2	0	
			1		

c)

		H	T	O	
		5	2	5	
	+		7	6	
		6	0	1	
			1	1	

4 Complete these additions.

a) $188 + 13 = \boxed{201}$

b) $50 + 672 = \boxed{722}$

c) $\boxed{500} = 39 + 461$

a)

		H	T	O	
		1	8	8	
	+		1	3	
		2	0	1	
			1	1	

b)

		H	T	O	
			5	0	
	+	6	7	2	
		7	2	2	
			1		

c)

		H	T	O	
			3	9	
	+	4	6	1	
		5	0	0	
			1	1	

5 Write each calculation in the correct column of the table.

238 + 71

827 + 31

712 + 38

318 + 72

731 + 28

73 + 182

No exchange	Exchange 10 ones	Exchange 10 tens
827+31	318+72	238+71
	712+38	

6 Find the missing digits.

a)

		H	T	O	
		3		5	
	+		6		
		4	1	6	

b)

		H	T	O	
		3	5		
	+			2	
		4	1	6	

7 Dana chooses a 2-digit number and a 3-digit number.

a) What is the greatest total she can make?

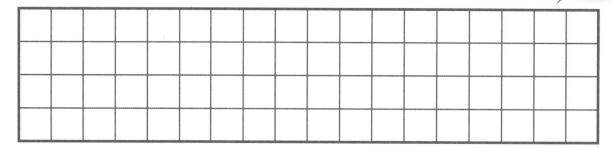

b) What is the smallest total she can make?

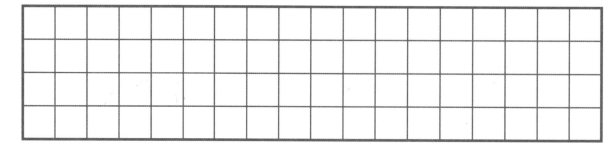

Reflect

What mistake has been made here?

Discuss with a partner why you need to be careful.

		H	T	O	
		1	4	7	
	+		3	2	

Date: 18.11.2022

Subtract a 2-digit number from a 3-digit number

1 Work out

a) 345 − 27 = 318

		H	T	O	
		3	³4	¹5	
	−		2	7	
		3	1	8	

b) 245 − 54 = 191

		H	T	O	
		¹2	¹4	5	
	−		5	4	
		1	9	1	

c) 412 − 38 = 374

		H	T	O	
		³4	¹⁰1	¹2	
	−		3	8	
		3	7	4	

2 Find 66 less than each number shown.

a)

		H	T	O	
		²3	¹4	7	
	−		6	6	
		2	8	1	

b)

		H	T	O	
		³4	¹5	6	
	−		6	6	
		3	9	0	

3 Complete these subtractions.

a)

		H	T	O	
		1 ~~7~~ 6	7	~~3~~	
–			4	5	
		1	2	8 ✓	

c) 231 – 62 = 169

		H	T	O	
		~~2~~ 1	~~3~~ 12	~~1~~ 11	
–			6	2	✓
		1	6	9	

b)

		H	T	O	
		2	~~6~~ 5	~~0~~ 10	
–			7	6	
		1	8	4	

d) 988 – 99 = 889

		H	T	O	
		~~8~~ 9	~~8~~ 17	~~8~~ 18	
–			9	9	
		8	8	9	✓

4 Look carefully at this calculation.

a) What mistake has been made?

<u>They didn't exchange the 7. ⓥ</u>

		H	T	O	
		1	5	7	
–			3	8	
		1	2	1	

b) Work out the correct answer.

		H	T	O	
		1	~~5~~ 4	~~7~~ 17	
–			3	8	
		2	0	0	✗
		1	1		

5 Use each digit card once to make one 2-digit number and one 3-digit number.

The numbers must have a difference of between 100 and 200.

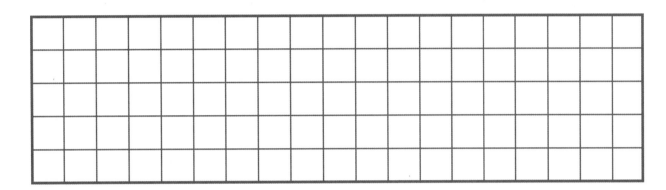

---

6 Crack the code. Each symbol represents one digit.

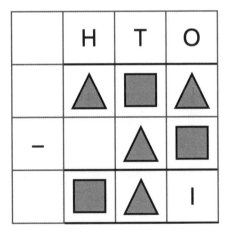

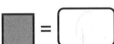 = [   ]

 = [7]

CHALLENGE

Reflect

Tell a partner something you have learnt about subtracting numbers with a different number of digits.

Date: 21.11.2022

Complements to 100

1

a) How many more squares does Cat have to move to get to 100?

25

b) How many more squares does Ball have to move to get to 100?

60 59

100	99	98	97	96	95	94	93	92	91
81	82	83	84	85	86	87	88	89	90
80	79	78	77	76		74	73	72	71
61	62	63	64	65	66	67	68	69	70
60	59	58	57	56	55	54	53	52	51
	42	43	44	45	46	47	48	49	50
40	39	38	37	36	35	34	33	32	31
21	22	23	24	25	26	27	28	29	30
20	19	18	17	16	15	14	13	12	11
1	2	3	4	5	6	7	8	9	10

2 Complete the number sentences.

a)

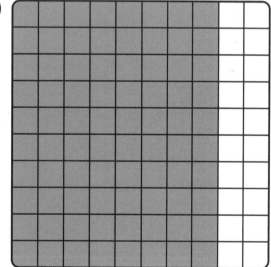

$80 + \boxed{20} = 100$

b)

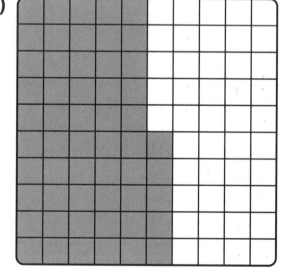

$55 + \boxed{45} = 100$

104

3 Work out the missing numbers.

a) $40 + \boxed{60} = 100$

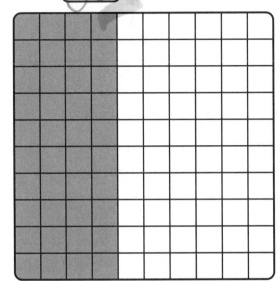

b) $\boxed{71} + 29 = 100$

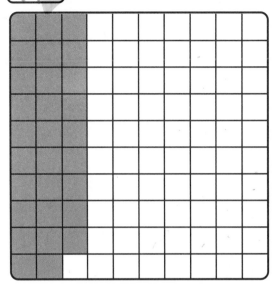

4 Complete the diagrams and number sentences.

a)

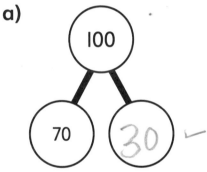

d) $7 + \boxed{93} = 100$

e) $\boxed{33} + 77 = 100$ Try this again
23 +

b)

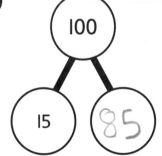

f) $100 = 100 + \boxed{0}$

c)

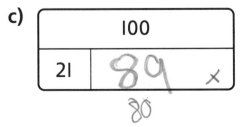

100	
21	89 ✗

80

I used a 100 square to help me.

105

5 Both numbers have the same value.

What is the value of each number?

| 40 | + | 60 | = 100

6 Fill in the missing digits in these number sentences.

CHALLENGE

a) 3☐ + 6·4 = 100

b) 4·5 + 5·5 = 100

4·6 + 5·9 = 100

4·7 + 5·3 = 100

c) 9·5 + 8☐ = 100

d) ☐6 + ☐4 = 100

☐6 + ☐4 = 100

☐6 + ☐4 = 100

Reflect

Write digits in the boxes to make the statement true.

☐0 + ☐0 = 100

How many different ways can you find?

Explain how you know you have found all the ways.

_____

_____

_____

Estimate answers

1 Work out an estimate for the answer to each calculation.

a) 304 + 198 = ⟨502⟩

My estimate:

⟨300⟩ + ⟨200⟩ = ⟨500⟩

b) 607 − 411 = ⟨196⟩

My estimate:

⟨600⟩ + ⟨400⟩ = ⟨1000⟩   *200*

c) 293 + 295 = ⟨ ⟩

My estimate:

⟨300⟩ + ⟨300⟩ = ⟨600⟩

d) 702 − 98 = ⟨ ⟩

My estimate:

⟨700⟩ − ⟨100⟩ = ⟨600⟩

2 Estimate the answer to each calculation.

Write the calculation and the estimate in the correct column of the table.

195 + 304	901 − 99	548 − 351

200 + 300 = 500   900 − 100 = 800   500 − 400 = 100

990 − 195	949 − 452	88 + 399

Approximately 200	Approximately 500	Approximately 800
	195 + 304 =	901 − 99

3 One of the children has made a mistake.

Estimate the answers to the calculations to find which one needs redoing.

a)

```
  H  T  O
  ⁴5̷ ¹⁰7̷ ¹2
-  2  8  9
   2  2  3
```

Lee

b)

```
  H  T  O
  3  0  2
+ 4  9  7
  7  9  9
```

Kate

c)

```
  H  T  O
  7  8  1
- 3  9  4
  3  1  3
```

Isla

Estimate [   ]   Estimate [   ]   Estimate [   ]

Use your estimates to decide whose calculation to redo.

Complete the calculation correctly.

		H	T	O	

4 Mo is is working out the answer to 147 + 539.

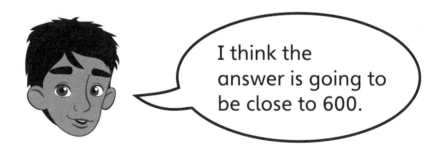

I think the answer is going to be close to 600.

a) Why do you think Mo thinks this? Discuss with a partner.

b) Find a better estimate for the answer. Explain your thinking.

_____

_____

5 Jamie and Andy are working out 198 + 297.

CHALLENGE

Jamie: I think the answer must be less than 500.

Andy: I will not know if it will be more or less than 500 until I do the calculation.

Who do you agree with?

I agree with _____ because _____

_____

_____

Reflect

Write an estimate for each calculation and then explain your reasoning.

205 + 198   513 − 308   448 + 297

[ ]   [ ]   [ ]

_____

_____

_____

Date: 30.11.2022

Inverse operations

1 Complete the calculations using fact families.

a)

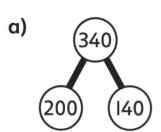

$200 = 340 - \boxed{140}$

$140 = 340 - \boxed{200}$

$\boxed{140} + 200 = \boxed{340}$

$200 + \boxed{140} = \boxed{340}$

b)

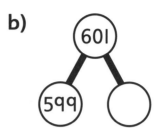

$601 - 599 = \boxed{2}$

$599 = 601 - \boxed{2}$

$599 + \boxed{2} = 601$

$601 = \boxed{2} + 599$

Discuss how you can use a fact family to help you check a calculation.

2 a) There is a mistake in the subtraction.

Complete the part-whole model and write an **addition** to check the subtraction.

$553 - 364 = 21$

	H	T	O	
	1	8	9	
+	3	6	4	
	5	5	3	
	1	1		

$$\begin{array}{r} 364 \\ -\ 21 \\ \hline \end{array}$$

b) Now complete the subtraction correctly.

	H	T	O	
	5	5	3	
–	3	6	4	
	1	8	9	

3 Complete the part-whole model.

Write an **addition** to check the subtraction.

517 − 310 = 207

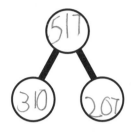

		H	T	O	
		3	1	0	
	+	2	0	7	
		5	1	7	

4 **a)** Write an **addition** to check Olivia's working.

I had 255 beads but I used 88 to make a necklace. Now I have 167 beads left.

		H	T	O					
			8	8					
	−		6	7					
		1	2	1					

b) I agree/~~disagree~~ with Olivia because it isn't 167 it

iss 121 and I know that because I did

a column subtraction.

5 **a)** Estimate the answer to 700 − 499.

CHALLENGE

b) Work out the answer using the column method.

		H	T	O	
	−				

c) Usman uses the number line to help him check the answer.

+1

499 500

Explain to a partner how you can check your answer.

_____

_____

Reflect

What different ways do you know for checking the answer to a question?

_____

_____

_____

Problem solving

1 **a)** Class 3 raised £125 and Class 4 raised £210.

How much did they raise altogether?

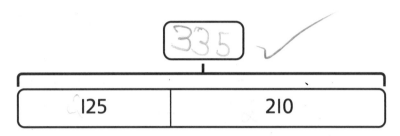

335

			H	T	O	
			2	1	0	
	+		1	2	5	
			3	3	5	

Class 3 and 4 raised £ altogether.

b) Class 5 have raised £231 so far. They are aiming for £325.

How much more do they need to raise?

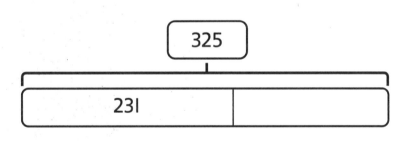

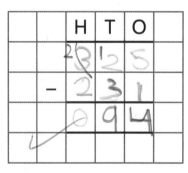

			H	T	O	
			²3	¹2	5	
	−		2	3	1	
			0	9	4	

They need to raise £ 94 more.

2 Dana and Luis are playing a game. Dana has scored 88 points and Luis has scored 175 points.

How many points have they scored altogether?

Draw a bar model to help you solve the problem.

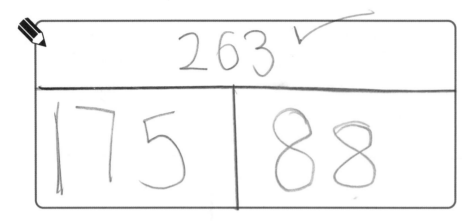

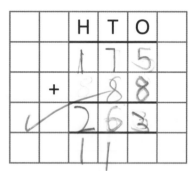

They have scored 263 points altogether. ✓

3 Rani has some shells. She adds 128 shells to her collection. Now she has 266 shells.

How many shells did she have to begin with?

Draw a bar model to help you solve the problem.

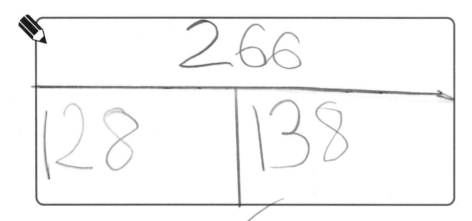

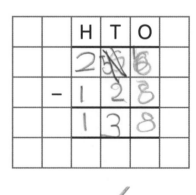

Ranie had 138 shells to begin with.

4

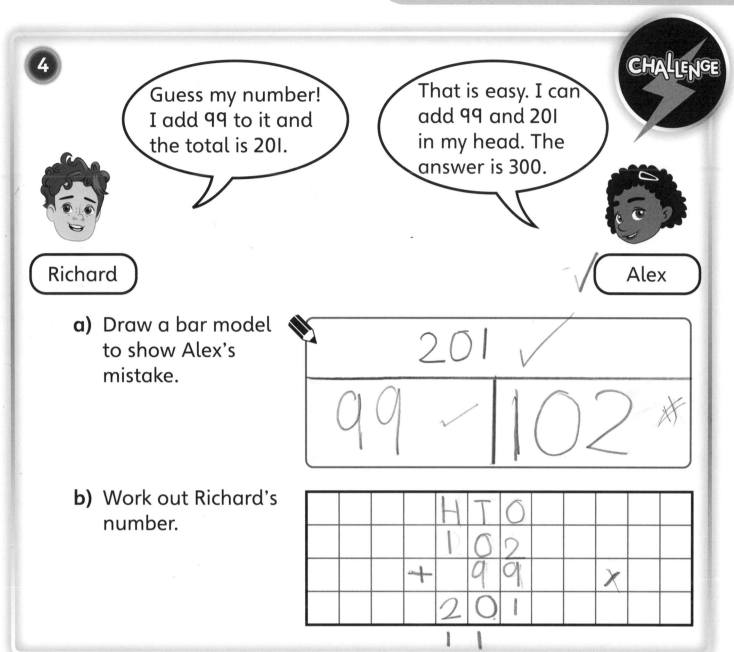

Guess my number! I add 99 to it and the total is 201.

That is easy. I can add 99 and 201 in my head. The answer is 300.

CHALLENGE

Richard

Alex ✓

a) Draw a bar model to show Alex's mistake.

201 ✓

99 ✓   102 ✗

b) Work out Richard's number.

Reflect

Write your own question to match the bar model.

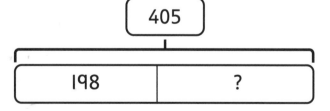

405

198	?

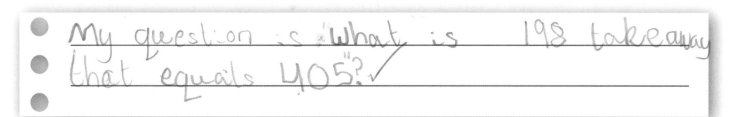

My question is "what is 198 takeaway that equals 405?" ✓

Date: 2.12.2022

Problem solving 2

1 There were 314 frogs in a pond in summer. By winter there were only 282 frogs. How many more frogs were there in the summer?

Summer | 314

Winter | 282 ⟷ ?

There were 32 more frogs in the summer.

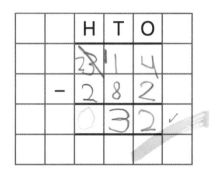

There were | 32 | more frogs in the summer.

2 Joshi spent £175 on his holiday. Jen spent £205.

a) Complete the bar model to show how much more Jen spent.

205

175 ⟷ ?

Jen spent £ 30 more than Joshi.

b) How much did they spend altogether?

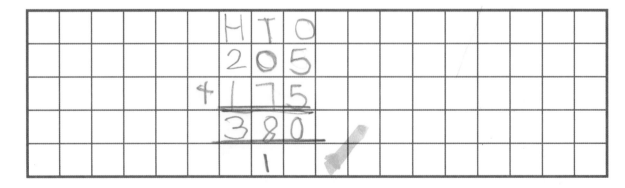

They spent £ [ ] altogether.

3 The Eiffel Tower is 324 m tall. The Blackpool Tower is 166 m shorter.

How tall is the Blackpool Tower?

Draw a bar model to help find the answer.

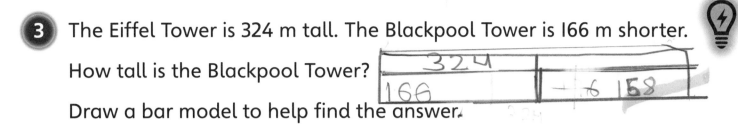

The Blackpool Tower is [176] m tall.

4 School A has 158 boys and 161 girls. School B has 173 boys and 118 girls.

Draw bar models to show each problem.

a) How many more girls than boys are there in School A?

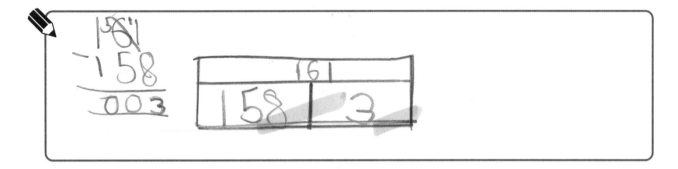

b) How many more children are there in School A than in School B?

117

5 Ebo thought of a number. Zac thought of a different number.

CHALLENGE

Complete the bar model to work out Ebo and Zac's numbers.

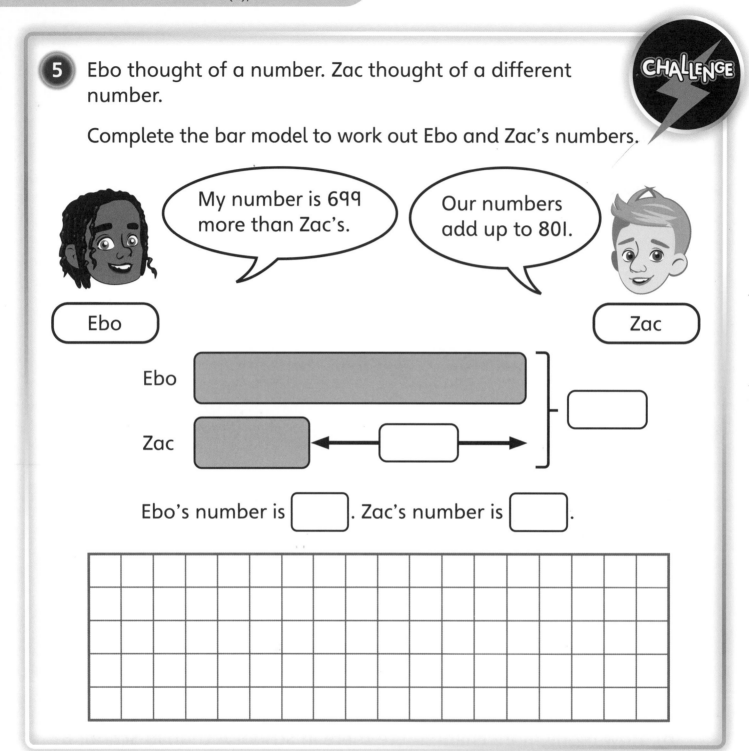

My number is 699 more than Zac's.

Our numbers add up to 801.

Ebo

Zac

Ebo

Zac

Ebo's number is ☐. Zac's number is ☐.

Reflect

Discuss with a partner when you would draw two bars and when you would draw one bar on a bar model.

→ Textbook 2A p160

End of unit check

My journal

Solve these calculations, then sort them from easiest to hardest.

Explain your decisions.

a)

301 − 199 = 102

b)

584 + 366 = 950

c)
995 − 671 = 324

d)
118 + 136 = 282

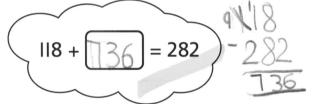
9⁄8'18
− 282
136

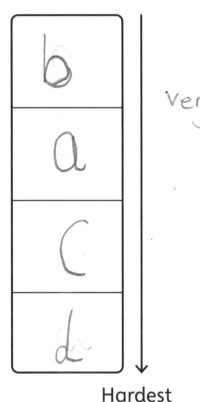

Easiest

b
a
c
d

Hardest

very good

Power check

How do you feel about your work in this unit?

Power play

Take it in turns with a partner to spin a 0–5 spinner.

Write each number you spin as one digit of your own addition.

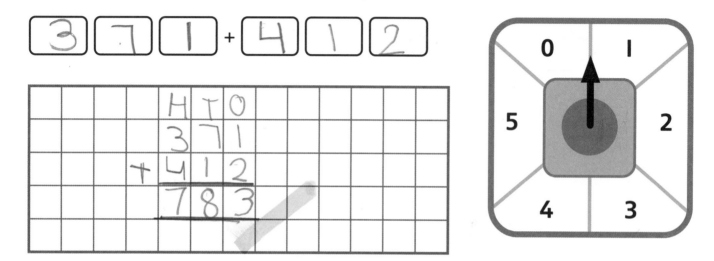

When your addition is complete, work out the answer and mark it on the number line.

Put 783 on the number line

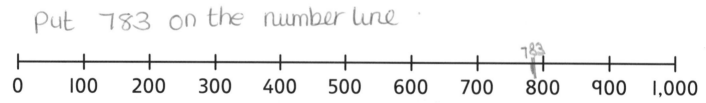

The aim is to get three answers in a row on the number line, without one of your partner's answers in between.

Change the challenge to see who can get an answer closest to a target number, such as 500.

Date: 6.12.2022

Multiplication – equal groups

1 Here are some apples.

a) Complete the sentences.

There are 3 bags of apples.

There are 5 apples in each group.

b) Write a multiplication for the total number of apples.

3 × 5 = 15

2 How many frogs are there in total?

4 × 2 = 8

3 How many buns are there?

a)

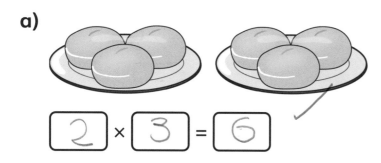

$$2 \times 3 = 6$$

b)

$$2 \times 4 = 8$$ ✓

c)

$$2 \times 5 = 10$$ ✓

4 Reena says these groups are not equal.

$3 \times 3 = 9$ ✓

Discuss this with a partner.

5 Match each multiplication to the addition.

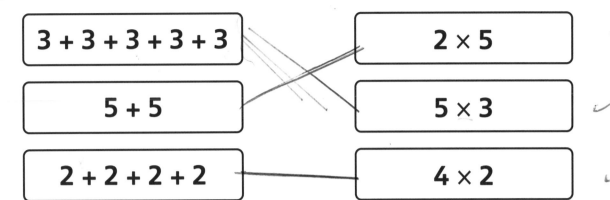

3 + 3 + 3 + 3 + 3	2 × 5
5 + 5	5 × 3
2 + 2 + 2 + 2	4 × 2

6 Take 20 cubes.

CHALLENGE

a) Show that you can make 10 equal groups of 2.

b) What other equal groups can you make using all the cubes?

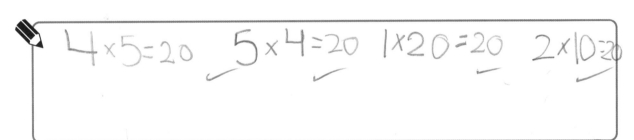

$4 \times 5 = 20$ $5 \times 4 = 20$ $1 \times 20 = 20$ $2 \times 10 = 20$

Reflect

Write down two things you know about equal groups.

_____

_____

Date: 4.1.2023

Use arrays

1 Write down two multiplications for each array.

a)

$5 \times 2 = 10$

$2 \times 5 = 10$

b)

$6 \times 2 = 12$

$2 \times 6 = 12$

c)

$3 \times 5 = 15$

$5 \times 3 = 15$

2 **a)** Draw or make an array of counters to show 4 × 5.

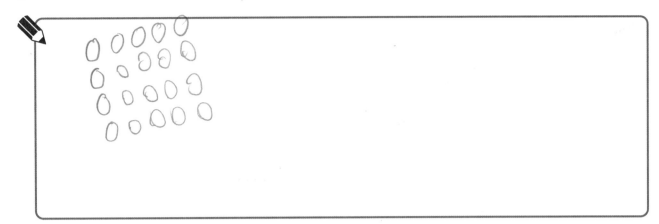

b) What other multiplication does your array show?

3 Here are some strawberries.

a) Circle 6 groups of 2.

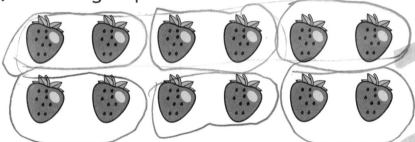

b) Circle 2 groups of 6.

c) Circle 4 groups of 3.

4 Here is part of a 2 × 3 array. Complete the array.

> I think there is more than one way of doing this.

CHALLENGE

5 **a)** What array can you see here?

b) Write two multiplications for your array.

$$\boxed{3} \times \boxed{6} = \boxed{18}$$ $$\boxed{6} \times \boxed{3} = \boxed{18}$$

Reflect

Draw or make your own array. Show a partner.

Ask your partner to write down two multiplications for your array.

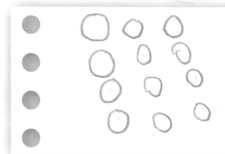

$$4 \times 3 = 12$$
$$3 \times 4 = 12$$

Multiplies of 2

→ Textbook 3A p172

1 Fill in the missing numbers.

a)

8	10	12	14	16	18	20	22	24	26

b)

24	26	28	30	32	34	36	38	40	42

c)

80	82	84	86	88	90	92	94	96	98

d)

50	48	46	44	42	40	38	36	34	32

2 Circle all the multiples of 2.

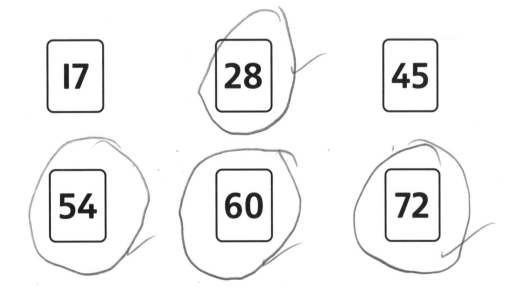

17   (28)   45

(54)   (60)   (72)

3　Colour in all the multiples of 2 that are greater than 50 but less than 75.

1	2	3	4	5	6	7	8	9	10
11	12	13	14	15	16	17	18	19	20
21	22	23	24	25	26	27	28	29	30
31	32	33	34	35	36	37	38	39	40
41	42	43	44	45	46	47	48	49	50
51	52	53	54	55	56	57	58	59	60
61	62	63	64	65	66	67	68	69	70
71	72	73	74	75	76	77	78	79	80
81	82	83	84	85	86	87	88	89	90
91	92	93	94	95	96	97	98	99	100

4　Ambika has made a 3-digit number.

She says her number is even.

What do you know about the last digit of Ambika's number?

Is It's an even number the last digit has to be either 0,2,4,6,or 8.

5 Here are three digit cards.

CHALLENGE

| 2 | 5 | 6 |

a) How many 2-digit even numbers can you make using these digit cards?

b) How many 2-digit odd numbers can you make?

c) How many 3-digit even numbers can you make?

Reflect

All multiples of 2 are even numbers.

Discuss this statement with a partner.

Date: 6.1.2023

Multiples of 5 and 10

1 Fill in the missing numbers.

a)

15	20	25	30	35	40	45	50

b)

75	80	85	90	95	100	105	115

c)

225	230	235	240	245	250	255	260

d)

50	45	40	35	30	25	20	15

2 Circle all the multiples of 5.

15   145   58

208   60   320

3 Is Kate correct?

390 is not a multiple of 5 as it does not end in a 5.

No Kate isn'tm correct because a multiple of 5 could be either 5, 10, 20, 15, 25, 30, 35, 40, 45. or 50.

4 Each of these numbers is a multiple of 5.

Complete the missing digits.

Write two answers for each one.

a) 52 0

  52 5

b) 3 0 5

  3 1 5

5 Write all the multiples of 5 that come between the two numbers shown on the number line.

273 275 280 285 290 295 315   320 322

_____

_____

_____

6

0   4   5

CHALLENGE

Arrange all the digit cards to make:

a) Two even multiples of 5. 20 30

b) Two odd multiples of 5. 25 35 ✓

c) Two numbers that are multiples of both 5 and 10. 50 60

Reflect

Sam says you can tell if a number is a multiple of 5 by looking at one of the digits.

Is Sam correct?

Yes because she can look at the ones column and if it ends in a 5 or 0.

Date: 9.1.2023

Share and group

1 Luis has 10 flowers.

He shares the flowers between 2 vases.

How many flowers are in each vase?

10 ÷ 2 = 5 ✓

2 Amelia has 10 flowers.

She puts the flowers into some vases.

She puts 2 flowers in each vase.

How many vases does she need?

10 ÷ 2 = 5 ✓

3 Take 20 counters.

a) Share the counters into 4 groups.

How many counters are in each group?

$\boxed{20} \div \boxed{5} = \boxed{4}$ ✓

b) Now put the counters into groups of 4.

How many groups did you make?

$\boxed{20} \div \boxed{4} = \boxed{5}$ ✓

c) Discuss what you notice with a partner.

4 Mrs Dean has £60.

She shares the amount equally between 5 friends.

a) How much do they get each?

$\boxed{60} \div \boxed{5} = \boxed{12}$ ✓

b) How much will each person get if she shares £60 equally between herself and her 5 friends?

$\boxed{60} \div \boxed{6} = \boxed{10}$ ✓ Super work.

$60 \div 6 = 10$

5 Take 12 cubes.

Make the following using all the cubes.

a) 2 equal towers $12 \div 6 = 2$ ✓

b) 3 equal towers $12 \div 4 = 3$ ✓

c) 4 equal towers $12 \div 3 = 4$ ✓

d) 5 equal towers $12 \div 2 = 5$ ✓

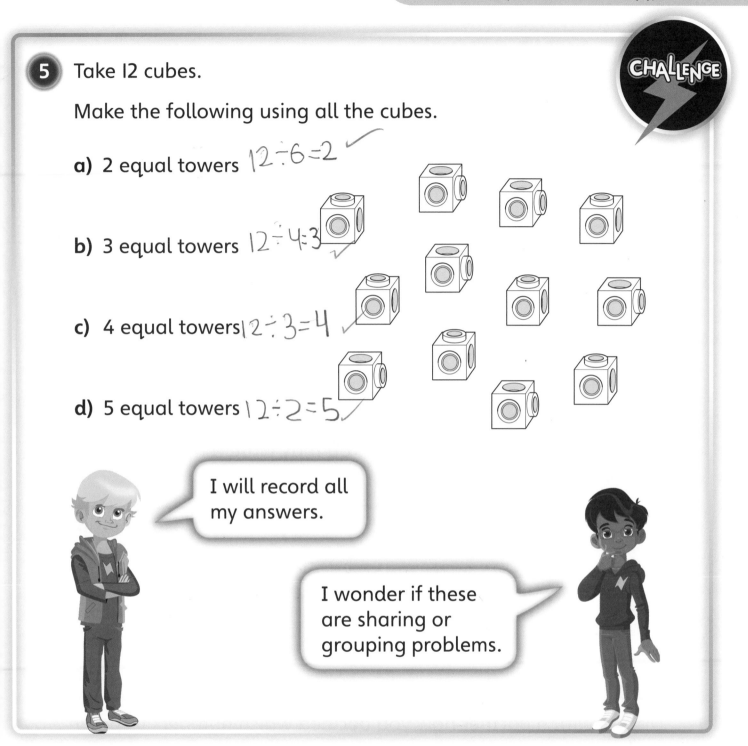

CHALLENGE

I will record all my answers.

I wonder if these are sharing or grouping problems.

Reflect

Discuss with a partner the difference between a sharing and a grouping problem.

135

Date: 10.1.2023

End of unit check

My journal

Let's see what you know about multiples of 2, 5 and 10.

Here are some numbers.

| 12 ✓ | 15 ✓ | 17 ✓ | 25 ✓ | 40 ✓ | 54 ✓ |

| 77 ✓ | 100 ✓ | 126 ✓ | 175 | 900 |

Sort the numbers into the table. You may write a number in more than one column.

Multiples of 2	Multiples of 5	Multiples of 10	Not multiples of 2, 5 or 10
12 40 54 100 126 900	15 25 40 100	40 100 900	17 75 25 40 5 00

Discuss with a partner how you decided which numbers to put in each column.

Power check

How do you feel about your work in this unit? ?

Power play

You will need: a team of 3 people and 3 piles of different coloured counters.

Each person chooses 1 colour of counter.

Player 1 must find all the multiples of 2.

Player 2 must find all the multiples of 5.

Player 3 must find all the multiples of 10.

Take it in turns to place 1 counter over your multiple.

Who can find all their multiples first?

1	2	3	4	5	6	7	8	9	10
11	12	13	14	15	16	17	18	19	20
21	22	23	24	25	26	27	28	29	30
31	32	33	34	35	36	37	38	39	40
41	42	43	44	45	46	47	48	59	50
51	52	53	54	55	56	57	58	59	60
61	62	63	64	65	66	67	68	69	70
71	72	73	74	75	76	77	78	79	80
81	82	83	84	85	86	87	88	89	90
91	92	93	94	95	96	97	98	99	100

When you have finished, write down how many even multiples of 5 you can find.

How many multiples of 2, 5 and 10 are there on the 100 square above?

How many even multiples of 5 are there?

Date: 11.1.2023

Multiply by 3

1 **a)** How many chairs are there in total?

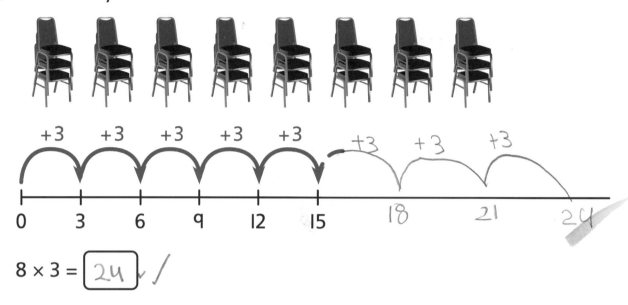

$8 \times 3 = \boxed{24}$ ✓ /

b) The roses are in bunches of 3. How many roses are there in total?

$\boxed{9} \times \boxed{3} = \boxed{27}$ ✓

2 A box contains 3 cakes.

Richard has 6 boxes of cakes.

How many cakes does Richard have?

$\boxed{6} \times \boxed{3} = \boxed{18}$ ✓

3 **a)** There are 12 marbles in each box.

How many marbles are there in total?

$\boxed{3} \times \boxed{12} = \boxed{36}$

b) Andy removes 2 marbles from each box.

How many marbles are there now?

$\boxed{3} \times \boxed{10} = \boxed{30}$

4 How many counters are there in total?

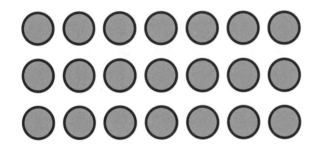 

I know the answer! I did it using two multiplications and then I added together.

I think there is a way of doing this with just one multiplication.

$\boxed{3} \times \boxed{11} = \boxed{33}$

5 12 × 3 = 36

Use this to help you work out 13 × 3.

Explain your method.

13 × 3 = [39]

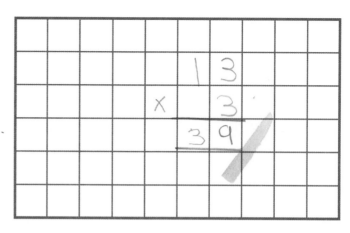

I did collumn times tables.

6 Do you think Danny is correct? Why?

> If you multiply an odd number by 3 you always get an odd number.

Danny

CHALLENGE

Yes because 3×7=21.

Reflect

The answer is 27. The working out is 9 × 3. Write a question that matches the working out and answer.

Date: 12.1.2023

Divide by 3

 a) 12 grapes are shared equally between 3 children.

How many grapes does each child get?

$12 \div 3 = \boxed{4}$

b) 15 balloons are tied into bundles of 3.

How many bundles can be made?

$\boxed{15} \div \boxed{3} = \boxed{5}$

c) 9 badges are shared equally between 3 people.

How many badges does each person get?

$\boxed{9} \div \boxed{3} = \boxed{3}$

141

2 **a)** Use the array to work out 27 ÷ 3.

27 ÷ 3 = **9**

b) Use the array to work out 18 ÷ 3.

18 ÷ 3 = **6**

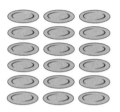

3 12 cubes are shared equally between 3 bags.

a) How many cubes are put into each bag? **4**

b) Can you share 13 cubes equally between 3 bags?

Explain your answer. Draw a diagram to help you.

I don't think I can share them equally.
If I cannot, I wonder how many more I need.

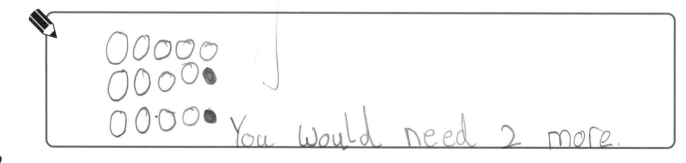

You would need 2 more.

4 $36 \div 3 = 12$

What is $42 \div 3$?

$42 \div 3 = \boxed{14}$ ✓

			3	6	÷	3	=	1	2		
		3	6		3	9			4	2	
		4	2	÷	3	=	1	4			

5 Here are some towers of cubes.

Andy uses the cubes to make towers 3 cubes high.

How many towers can he make? $\boxed{6}$ ✓

CHALLENGE

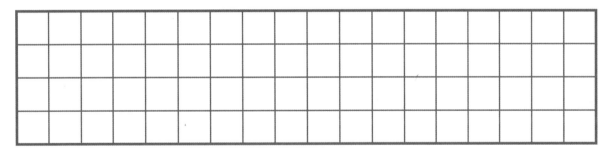

Reflect

Explain how you would work out that $15 \div 3 = 5$.

_____

_____

_____

Date: 13.1.2023

The 3 times-table

1 Which 3 times-table fact does each picture show?

a)

$\boxed{3} \times \boxed{5} = \boxed{15}$ ✓

b)

$\boxed{3} \times \boxed{10} = \boxed{30}$ ✓

c)

$\boxed{3} \times \boxed{4} = \boxed{12}$ ✓

2 Work out these multiplications.

a) $0 \times 3 = \boxed{0}$ ✓

c) $\boxed{21} = 7 \times 3$ ✓

b) $9 \times 3 = \boxed{27}$ ✓

d) $\boxed{8} \times 3 = 24$ ✓

3 Join the calculations to the correct circle. Complete any calculations that are already joined to a circle.

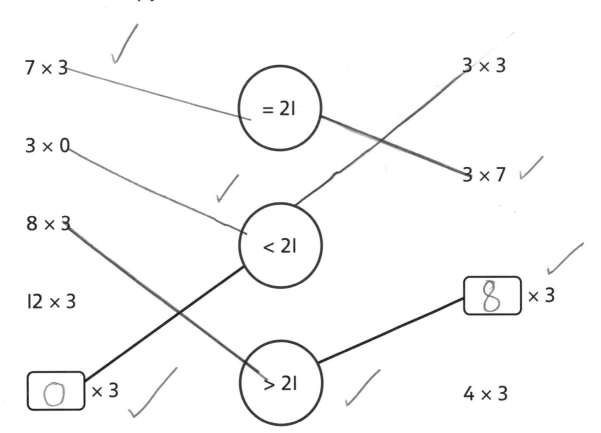

7 × 3 ✓

3 × 0

8 × 3

12 × 3

$\boxed{0}$ × 3 ✓

= 21

< 21 ✓

> 21 ✓

3 × 3

3 × 7 ✓

$\boxed{8}$ × 3 ✓

4 × 3

4 Work out these divisions.

a) $36 \div 3 = \boxed{12}$ ✓

b) $18 \div 3 = \boxed{6}$ ✓

c) $21 \div 3 = \boxed{7}$ ✓

d) $0 \div 3 = \boxed{0}$ ✓

e) $\boxed{12} \div 3 = 4$ ✓

f) $\boxed{1} \div 3 = 1$ ✗

g) $15 \div \boxed{3} = 5$ ✓

h) $\boxed{30} \div 3 = 10$ ✓

145

5 Complete using <, > or =.

a) 5×3 ⟨>⟩ 8 ✓

b) 3×7 ⟨>⟩ 20 ✓

c) 5×3 ⟨=⟩ 3×5 ✓

d) 4×3 ⟨<⟩ 3×6 ✓

e) $12 \div 3$ ⟨<⟩ 9 ✓

f) $33 \div 3$ ⟨>⟩ 10 ✓

g) $15 \div 3$ ⟨<⟩ $18 \div 3$ ✓

h) 9×3 ⟨>⟩ $9 \div 3$ ✓

I wonder if you always have to work out the calculations.

6 Colour in all the numbers in the 3 times-table.

What patterns do you notice?

Discuss with a partner the patterns you can see.

1	2	3	4	5	6	7	8	9	10
11	12	13	14	15	16	17	18	19	20
21	22	23	24	25	26	27	28	29	30
31	32	33	34	35	36	37	38	39	40
41	42	43	44	45	46	47	48	49	50
51	52	53	54	55	56	57	58	59	60
61	62	63	64	65	66	67	68	69	70
71	72	73	74	75	76	77	78	79	80
81	82	83	84	85	86	87	88	89	90
91	92	93	94	95	96	97	98	99	100

CHALLENGE

Reflect

Roll two dice. Add the two numbers together and multiply your answer by 3.

See how many times you can do this in 1 minute. Go!

Date: 31.1.2023

Multiply by 4

1 **a)** How many muffins are there?

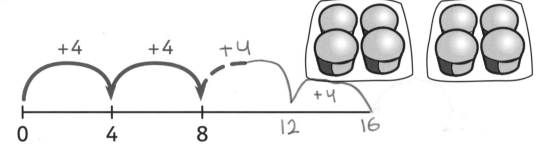

$$\boxed{5} \times \boxed{4} = \boxed{20}$$

b) How many glasses are there?

$$\boxed{9} \times \boxed{4} = \boxed{36}$$

2 Max draws squares and counts the sides.

Complete the table.

Number of squares	0	1	2	5	8	11	12
Number of sides	0	4	8	20	32	44	48

147

3 A plank is 4 metres long.

What is the total length of all the planks?

$6 \times 4 = 24$

4 The prices of a mug and a teddy bear are shown.

£5   £4

a) Aki buys 7 teddy bears.

What is the total cost?

$7 \times 4 = 28$

b) Aki also buys 4 mugs.

What is the total cost of the mugs?

$4 \times 5 = 20$

c) How much does Aki spend in total?

$28 + 20 = 48$

5 Use Olivia's rule to multiply these numbers by 4.

a) 21 _42 64 128_

b) 50 _____

c) 27 _____

> To multiply by 4, you can double and then double again.

6 There are 4 cards in a pack.

Ali buys 7 packs. Mark buys 5 packs.

How many cards do they have altogether? ☐

CHALLENGE

Reflect

How do you multiply a number by 4?

- _____
- _____
- _____

Date: _____

Divide by 4

1 **a)** 12 jelly beans are shared equally between 4 children.

How many beans does each child get?

12 ÷ 4 = ☐

b) Apples are packed into boxes of 4.

How many boxes of apples can be made?

☐ ÷ ☐ = ☐

2 Liam counts 20 legs on a group of cats.

How many cats are there?

☐ ÷ ☐ = ☐

3 Use the array to work out 32 ÷ 4.

32 ÷ 4 = ☐

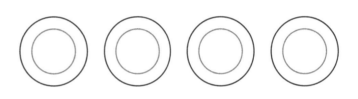

4 28 biscuits are shared equally between 4 plates.

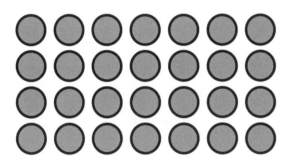

How many biscuits are there on each plate?

☐ ○ ☐ = ☐

5 A magazine costs £4.

How many magazines can Richard buy with this note?

☐ ○ ☐ = ☐

6 Is Jamilla correct? Explain your answer.

I think 24 divided by 4 is greater than 24 divided by 3 because 4 is a bigger number.

_____

_____

7 Use Lee's fact to divide 64 by 4.

CHALLENGE

To divide a number by 4 you can halve it and halve it again.

_____

_____

Reflect

Draw a picture that explains why dividing by 4 is the same as dividing by 2 and dividing by 2 again.

Date: _____

The 4 times-table

→ Textbook 3A p208

1 Which fact from the 4 times-table does each picture show?

a)

$\boxed{} \times \boxed{} = \boxed{}$

b)

$\boxed{} \times \boxed{} = \boxed{}$

c)

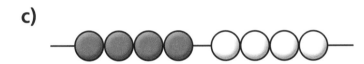

$\boxed{} \times \boxed{} = \boxed{}$

2 Complete the multiplications.

a) $5 \times 4 = \boxed{}$

b) $\boxed{} = 1 \times 4$

c) $4 \times 9 = \boxed{}$

d) $4 \times 3 = \boxed{}$

e) $\boxed{} \times 4 = 28$

f) $\boxed{} \times 4 = 44$

g) $0 = \boxed{} \times 4$

h) $48 = 12 \times \boxed{}$

3 **a)** Circle the numbers that are in the 4 times-table.

16   20   48   11   28   0   52   40   400

b) Explain how Andy knows this so quickly.

I know straight away that 11 is not in the 4 times-table.

_____

_____

c) Is Zac correct?

Convince a partner.

I don't think 400 is in the 4 times-table. It stops at 48.

4 Complete the missing numbers to make the calculations correct.

a) $36 \div 4 = \boxed{}$

e) $\boxed{} = 20 \div 4$

b) $28 \div 4 = \boxed{}$

f) $\boxed{} = 32 \div 4$

c) $40 \div 4 = \boxed{}$

g) $\boxed{} \div 4 = 3$

d) $8 \div 4 = \boxed{}$

h) $\boxed{} \div 4 = 11$

5 Complete using <, > or =.

a) $2 \times 4 \bigcirc 6$

b) $9 \times 4 \bigcirc 10 \times 4$

c) $8 \times 3 \bigcirc 6 \times 4$

d) $20 \div 4 \bigcirc 16$

e) $40 \div 4 \bigcirc 10$

f) $12 \div 4 \bigcirc 24 \div 4$

6 Work out the missing numbers.

CHALLENGE

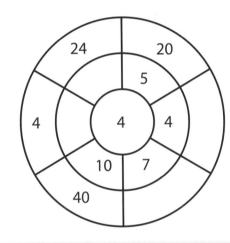

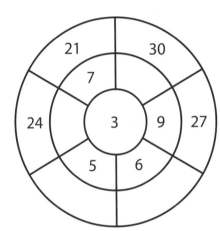

Reflect

12 is in the 3 times-table and the 4 times-table.

Find some other numbers that are in both the 3 and the 4 times-tables.

Is there a pattern?

155

Date: 19.1.2023   FN

Multiply by 8

1 **a)** How many pens are there altogether?

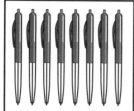 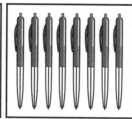 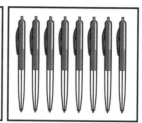

$$\boxed{3} \times \boxed{8} = \boxed{24}$$

b) How many flowers are there?

$$\boxed{6} \times \boxed{8} = \boxed{48}$$

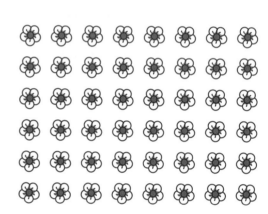

2 A spider has 8 legs.

How many legs do 5 spiders have?

$$\boxed{5} \times \boxed{8} = \boxed{40}$$

3 What is the mass of the dog?

$$\boxed{7} \times \boxed{8} = \boxed{56}$$

4 There are some biscuits in 4 jars.

How many biscuits are there in total?

$4 \times 8 = 32$ ✓

5 a) Lexi multiplied her number by 4 and got 28.

What is Lexi's number multiplied by 8? 56 ✓

b) If ☆ × 8 = 64, what is ☆ × 4? 32 ✓

6 Here is a rule for multiplying 12 by 8.

> ### To multiply 12 by 8
>
> First, double 12, which is 24.
>
> Next, double 24, which is 48.
>
> Then double 48, which is 96.
>
> So, 12 × 8 = 96.

Use the same rule to work out the multiplications.

a) 20 multiplied by 8.

20 × 8 = ☐

b) 37 multiplied by 8.

37 × 8 = ☐

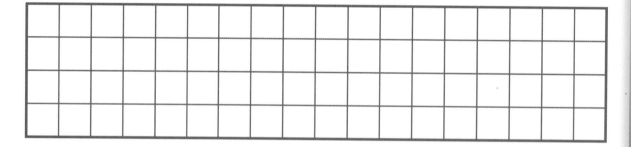

Reflect

If you know that 6 × 4 = 24, how can you work out 6 × 8?

Explain your answer.

You would need to double 24.
24×2=48

Date: 20.1.2023

Divide by 8

→ Textbook 3A p216

1 **a)** Pegs are packed into packs of 8.

There are 24 pegs.

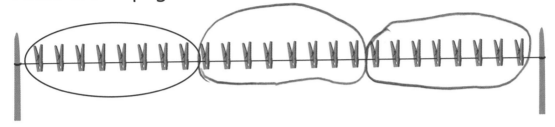

How many packs are made?

24 ÷ 8 = 3 ✓ ✓

b) A lorry has 8 wheels.

How many lorries are there?

32 ÷ 8 = 4 ✓ ✓

2 8 balls are shared equally between 8 cats.

How many balls does each cat get?

8 ÷ 8 = 1 ✓ ✓

159

3 Millie draws some octagons.

An octagon has 8 sides. Millie draws 48 sides in total.

How many octagons does she draw?

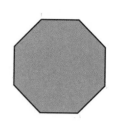

$\boxed{48} \div \boxed{8} = \boxed{6}$ ✓

4 Use the diagrams to help you work out the divisions.

a)

$16 \div 4 = \boxed{4}$ ✓ $16 \div 8 = \boxed{2}$ ✓

b)

£40 ÷ 4 = $\boxed{10}$ ✓   £40 ÷ 8 = $\boxed{5}$ ✓

5 A bag of counters is shared equally between 8 children.

Each child receives 4 counters.

How many counters were in the bag?

 $\boxed{8} \div \boxed{4} = \boxed{2}$ ✗

6 Jamie divides her number by 8.

What answer does she get?

Show your working.

When I divide my number by 4, I get 6.

CHALLENGE

Reflect

Write or draw the steps to work out 16 divided by 8.

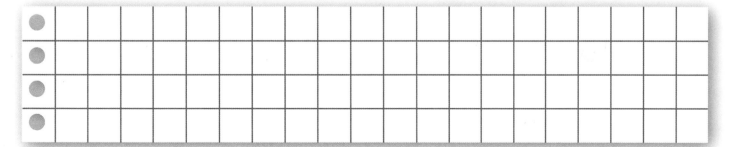

Date: 23.1.2023

The 8 times-table

1 Which 8 times-table fact does each picture show?

a)

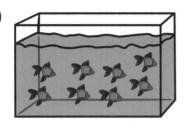 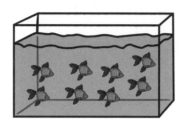

$\boxed{2} \times 8 = \boxed{16}$ ✓

b)

$\boxed{1} \times \boxed{8} = \boxed{8}$ ✓

c)

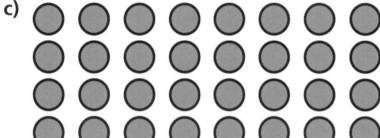

$\boxed{4} \times \boxed{8} = \boxed{32}$ ✓

2 Work out

a) $6 \times 8 = \boxed{48}$ ✓

b) $0 \times 8 = \boxed{0}$ ✓

c) $\boxed{96} = 12 \times 8$ ✓

d) $5 \times 8 = \boxed{40}$ ✓

e) $\boxed{80} = 8 \times 10$ ✓

f) $64 = 8 \times \boxed{8}$ ✓

g) $\boxed{1} \times 8 = 8$ ✗

h) $\boxed{7} \times 8 = 56$ ✓

162

3 Fill in the missing numbers.

a)

| 8 | 16 | 24 | 32 | 40 | 48 | 56 |

b)

| 96 | 88 | 80 | 72 | 64 | 56 | 48 | 40 |

c)

| 40 | 48 | 56 | 64 | 72 | 80 |

d)

| 40 | 32 | 24 | 16 | 8 | 0 |

4 Work out the missing numbers.

a) $40 \div 8 = \boxed{5}$ ✓

b) $\boxed{3} = 24 \div 8$ ✓

c) $32 \div 8 = \boxed{4}$ ✓

d) $\boxed{12} = 96 \div 8$ ✓

e) $\boxed{9} = 72 \div 8$ ✓

f) $\boxed{80} \div 8 = 10$ ✓

g) $\boxed{8} \div 8 = 1$ ✓

h) $\boxed{0} \div 8 = 0$ ✓

5 Complete the sentences using <, > or =.

a) 2×8 ⟨$>$⟩ 10 ^16 ✓

b) 5×8 ⟨$<$⟩ 6×8 ^40 ^43 ✓

c) 4×8 ⟨$=$⟩ 8×4 ^32 ^32 ✓

d) $32 \div 8$ ⟨$=$⟩ 4 ^4 ✓

e) $40 \div 8$ ⟨$<$⟩ 20 ^5 ✓

f) $16 \div 8$ ⟨$<$⟩ $8 \div 4$ ^2   ^(32) ^2 JM

you x instead of ÷
=

163

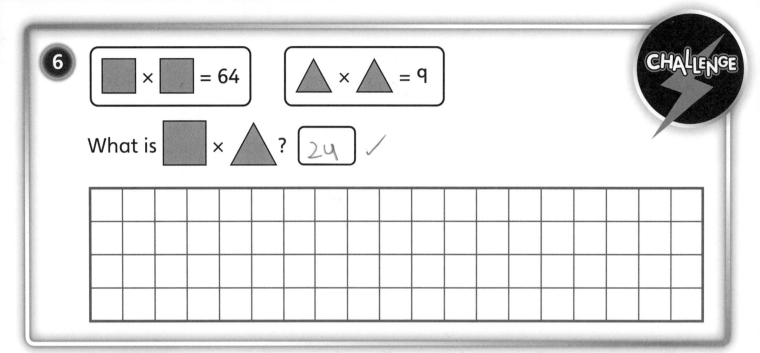

6 ▢ × ▢ = 64   △ × △ = 9

What is ▢ × △ ? 24 ✓

CHALLENGE

Reflect

How many times-table facts can you write in this table?

Some have been done for you.

The answer is 0	The answer is greater than 30, but less than 40	The answer is 40	The answer is greater than 70
$0 \times 3 = 0$	$4 \times 8 = 32$	$2 \times 20 = 40$	$10 \times 9 = 90$

What do you notice about the numbers in the facts in the first column?

- _____
- _____
- _____

Problem solving – multiplication and division

1 **a)** What is the total score?

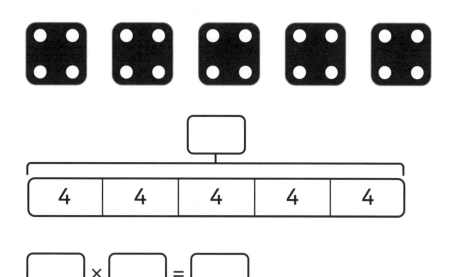

$$\boxed{} \times \boxed{} = \boxed{}$$

b) There are 8 rulers in each box. How many rulers are there?

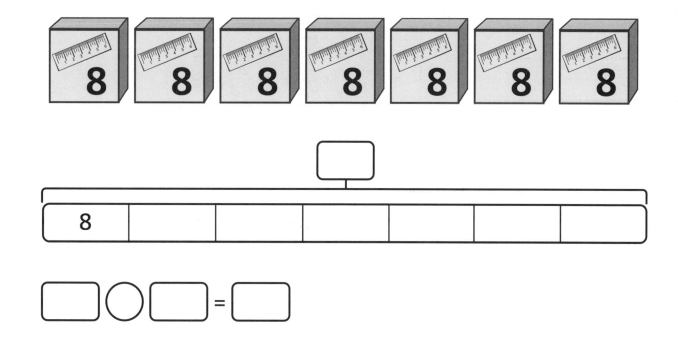

$$\boxed{} \bigcirc \boxed{} = \boxed{}$$

2 16 flowers are divided equally between 4 pots.

How many flowers are in each pot?

$\boxed{} \div \boxed{} = \boxed{}$

3 These buttons are put into bags of 8.

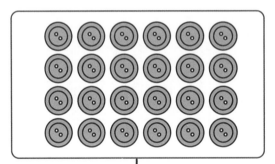

How many bags are needed?

$\boxed{} \bigcirc \boxed{} = \boxed{}$

4 A game costs £3.

Marcus buys 5 games.

How much do 5 games cost in total?

Draw a bar model.

Write the calculation.

⬚ ◯ ⬚ = ⬚

5 How much does each box weigh? ⬚ kg

CHALLENGE

Reflect

Aki is solving a multiplication word problem. The answer is 24.

What could the question be?

_____

_____

_____

_____

Date: 25.1.2023

Problem solving – multiplication and division ❷

1 **a)** How many jam tarts are on each tray?

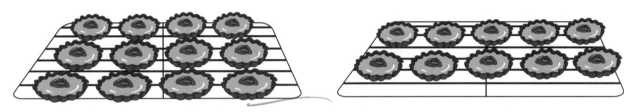

 $\boxed{3} \times \boxed{4} = \boxed{12}$

 $\boxed{2} \times \boxed{5} = \boxed{10}$

b) How many jam tarts are there in total?

$\boxed{12} + \boxed{10} = \boxed{22}$

2 How many counters are there in total?

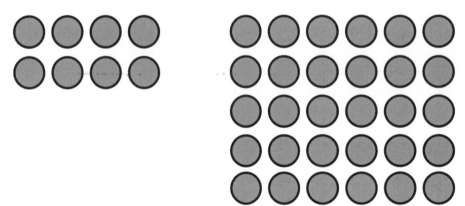

	2	$\times$	4	$=$	8		5	$\times$	6	$=$	3	0					
	8	$+$	3	0	$=$	3	8										

There are $\boxed{38}$ counters in total.

3

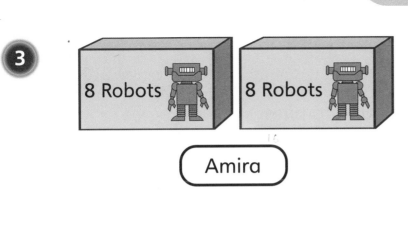

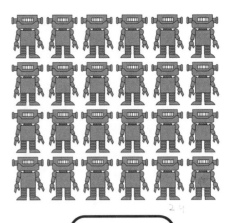

a) Who has more robots?

J	a	m	i	e		h	a	s		t	h	e		m	o	s	t	.									
			8	×	2		=	1		6						8		×	3		=	2		4			

_____Jamie ✓_____ has more robots.

b) How many more robots do they have?

J	a	m	i	e		h	a	s		8		m	o	r	e		t	h	a	n		A	m	i	r	a	.		

They have ⬜ 8 more robots.

4 **a)** How much do 7 buckets cost altogether?

⬚ 7 ⊗ ⬚ 3 = ⬚ 21

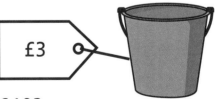

£3

b) How many beach balls can you buy with £40?

⬚ 40 ⊖ ⬚ 8 = ⬚ 5

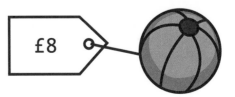

£8

5 Cards come in boxes of 10.

The cards from 6 boxes are put into piles.

There are 4 cards in each pile.

How many piles of 4 cards can be made?

CHALLENGE

$10 \times 4 = 40$ $\quad$ $5 \times 4 = 20$

$15 \times 4 = 60$ $\quad$ 60

15 piles of 4 cards can be made.

Reflect

Make up a multiplication or division question about this price list.

Challenge a partner to answer it.

Coffee £2 $\qquad$ Sandwich £4

Muffin £3 $\qquad$ Cake £8.

£9 + £8 = £17 $\times$ $\qquad$ 10 cakes will cost $10 \times 8 = 80$.

170

Understand divisibility ❶

1 Lexi has 11 lollipop sticks.

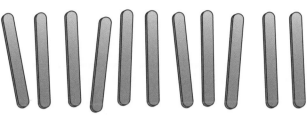

She makes squares, like this.

a) Draw the squares that Lexi makes.

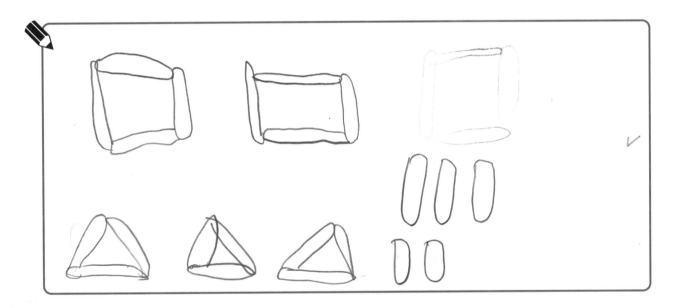

b) How many complete squares can Lexi make? ☐ 2 ✓

c) What is the remainder? ☐ 3 ✓ ✓

d) How many complete triangles can Lexi make with 11 sticks? ☐ 3 ✓

What is the remainder? ☐ 2 ✓ ✓

2 Now Lexi is using lollipop sticks to make pentagons.

a) Complete the table.

Lollipop sticks	Working	Number of pentagons	Remainder
12		2	2
13		2	3 ✓
14		2 ✓	4 ✓
15		3 ✓✓	0 ✓
16		3 ✓	1 ✓
23 ✓		4	3

b) What is the greatest number of lollipop sticks that can be left over? Explain why.

4 ✓ because Lolli...

3 Max makes square blocks from cubes, like this.

He makes 5 square blocks and has a remainder of 3 cubes.

CHALLENGE

How many cubes did Max start with? ☐

Reflect

Why is Aki correct?

Discuss with a partner.

When you divide by 5, the greatest remainder is 4.

Date: _27.1.2023_

Understand divisibility ❷

1   Share 7 cakes between 2 plates.

a)   How many cakes are on each plate?   ☐ 3 ✓

b)   How many are left over?   ☐ 1 ✓

c)   Work out 7 ÷ 2 = ☐ 3 remainder ☐ 1 .

2   7 cakes are packed into boxes of 3.

a)   Circle the groups of 3.

b)   How many complete boxes are there?   ☐ 2 ✓

c)   How many cakes are left over?   ☐ 1

d)   Work out 7 ÷ 3 = ☐ 2 remainder ☐ 1 . ✓

3 These apples are shared between 4 children.

How many apples does each child get?

How many apples are left over?

$9 \div 4 =$ [2] remainder [1] ✓

4 Use counters to work out the divisions.

a) $15 \div 2 =$ [7] remainder [1] ✓

b) $15 \div 3 =$ [5] remainder [1] ✗

c) $15 \div 4 =$ [4] remainder [0] ✗

d) $15 \div 5 =$ [3] remainder [1] ✗

e) $15 \div 6 =$ [2] remainder [4] ✗

5 Look at these calculations.

Circle the three that will have a remainder.

Discuss with a partner how you know.

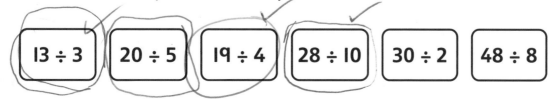

$13 \div 3$ $20 \div 5$ $19 \div 4$ $28 \div 10$ $30 \div 2$ $48 \div 8$

175

6 **a)** When I divide a number by 4, the remainder is 1.

What could the number be?

Find three possible numbers.

29 : 4 =

_____

b) When Jamie divides her number by 5, the remainder is 7.

How do you know that Jamie has made a mistake?

_____

_____

7 Work out the missing number.

$\boxed{} \div 5 = 4$ remainder 4

Reflect

What is the remainder when each of these numbers is divided by 3?

3, 6, 9, 12, 15, 18, 21, 24, 27, 30

How do you know?

What numbers will give a remainder of 1 when you divide by 3?

- _____
- _____
- _____

End of unit check

My journal

You now know the 2, 3, 4, 5, 8 and 10 times-tables.

Work out a number that could go into each box.

What strategy did you use?

	My number
a) A number in the 2 and 5 times-tables greater than 25	30
b) A number in the 3, 4 and 8 times-tables	24
c) A number in the 8 and 10 times-tables less than 50	40
d) A number in the 3, 4 and 5 times-tables	

Power check

How do you feel about your work in this unit?   ?

Power play

Time trial

a) How quickly can you complete these times-table wheels?

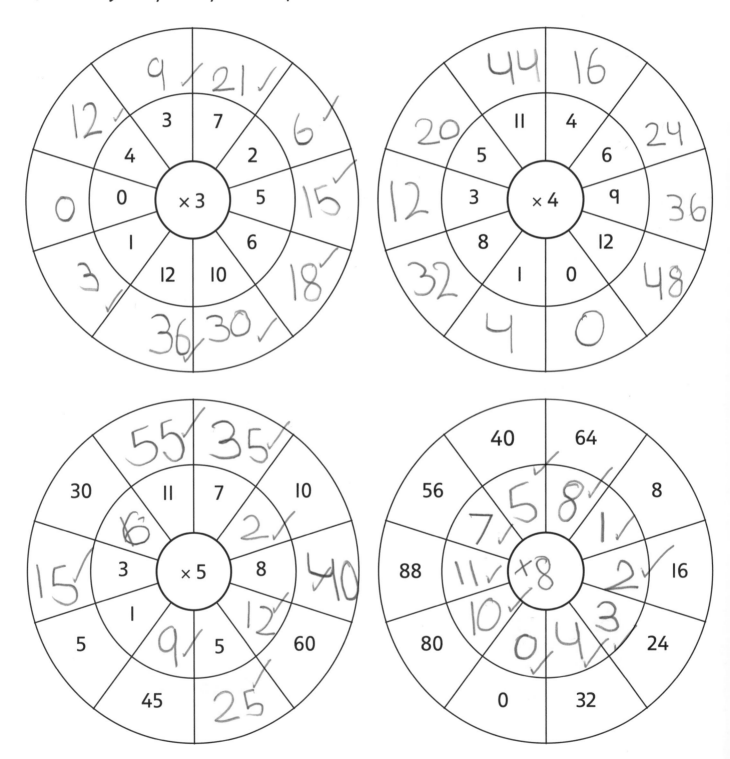

b) This is a different type of wheel. Can you find the missing numbers?

You can only use the 2, 3, 4, 5, 8 and 10 times-tables.

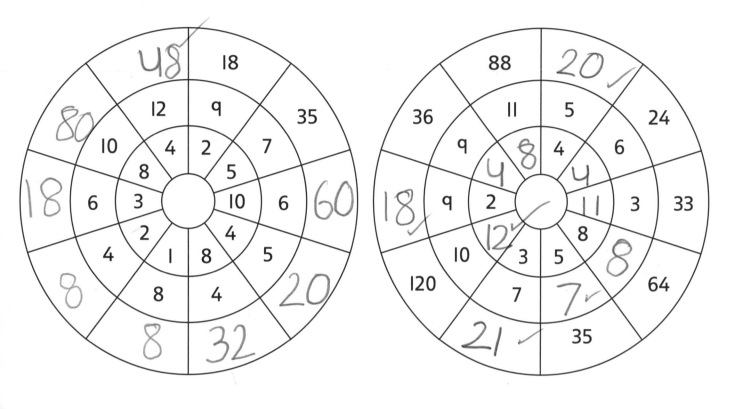

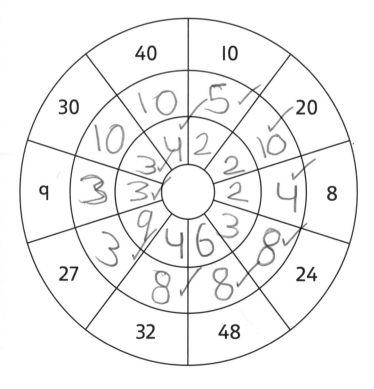

Can you make up your own wheels to challenge a partner?

My power points

Colour in the ☆ to show what you have learnt.

Colour in the ☺ if you feel happy about what you have learnt.

Unit I

I can …

☆ ☺ Count in 100s

☆ ☺ Partition a number in 100s, 10s and Is

☆ ☺ Find I, 10 and 100 more or less

☆ ☺ Compare and order numbers up to 1,000

☆ ☺ Count in 50s

Unit 2

I can …

☆ ☺ Use number bonds within 10

☆ ☺ Add and subtract Is, 10s and 100s

☆ ☺ Add and subtract Is and 10s across 100

☆ ☺ Explain when to exchange Is, 10s and 100s

☆ ☺ Add and subtract using mental and written methods

Unit 3

I can …

☆ ☺ Add and subtract 3-digit numbers

☆ ☺ Decide when I need to exchange

☆ ☺ Exchange across more than one column

☆ ☺ Check my answers in different ways

☆ ☺ Use bar models to solve 1- and 2-step problems

Unit 4

I can …

☆ ☺ Recognise unequal groups

☆ ☺ Understand how an array can show two multiplications

☆ ☺ Work out multiples of 2, 5 and 10

Unit 5

I can …

☆ ☺ Say the 3, 4, and 8 times-tables

☆ ☺ Find a simple remainder when a number is divided

☆ ☺ Use a bar model to solve multiplication and division problems

Keep up the good work!

Published by Pearson Education Limited, 80 Strand, London, WC2R 0RL.

www.pearsonschools.co.uk

Text © Pearson Education Limited 2018, 2022
Edited by Pearson and Florence Production Ltd
First edition edited by Pearson, Little Grey Cells Publishing Services and Haremi Ltd
Designed and typeset by Pearson and Florence Production Ltd
First edition designed and typeset by Kamae Design
Original illustrations © Pearson Education Limited 2018, 2022
Illustrated by Nigel Dobbyn, Virginia Fontanabona, Paul Moran, Nadene Naude at Beehive
Illustration, Emily Skinner at Graham-Cameron Illustration, Florence Production Ltd and
Kamae Design
Images: Bank of England: 151
Cover design by Pearson Education Ltd
Front and back cover illustrations by Diego Diaz and Nadene Naude at Beehive Illustration
Series editor: Tony Staneff; Lead author: Josh Lury
Authors (first edition): Tony Staneff and Josh Lury
Consultants (first edition): Professor Liu Jian and Professor Zhang Dan

The rights of Tony Staneff and Josh Lury to be identified as authors of this work have been
asserted by them in accordance with the Copyright, Designs and Patents Act 1988.

First published 2018
This edition first published 2022

26 25 24 23 22
10 9 8 7 6 5 4 3 2 1

British Library Cataloguing in Publication Data
A catalogue record for this book is available from the British Library

ISBN 978 1 292 41942 8

Printed in the UK by Bell & Bain Ltd, Glasgow

For Power Maths online resources, go to:
www.activelearnprimary.co.uk

Note from the publisher
Pearson has robust editorial processes, including answer and fact checks, to ensure the accuracy of
the content in this publication, and every effort is made to ensure this publication is free of errors.
We are, however, only human, and occasionally errors do occur. Pearson is not liable for any
misunderstandings that arise as a result of errors in this publication, but it is our priority to ensure
that the content is accurate. If you spot an error, please do contact us at resourcescorrections@
pearson.com so we can make sure it is corrected.